# CLEAR
# TECHNICAL
# WRITING

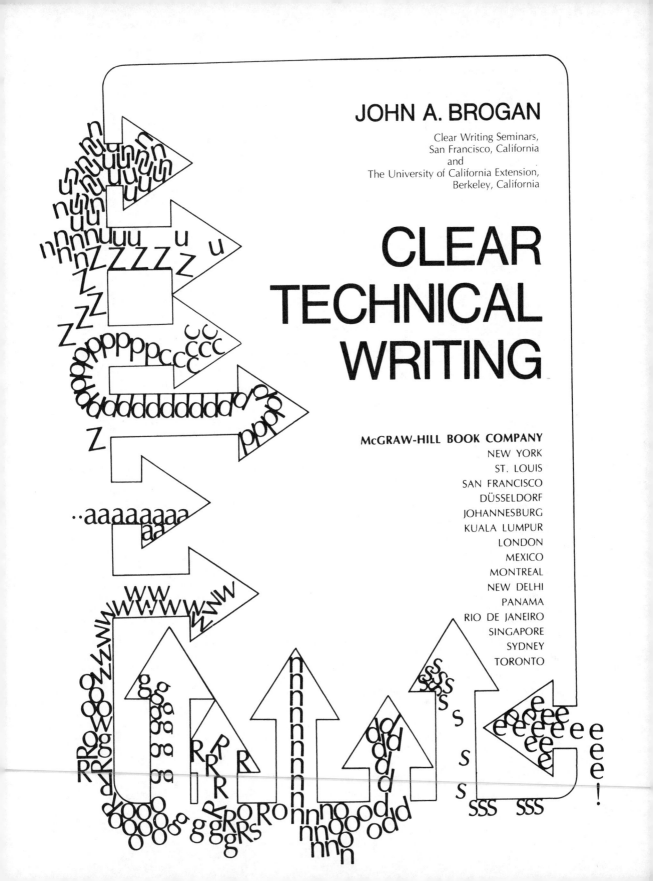

JOHN A. BROGAN

Clear Writing Seminars,
San Francisco, California
and
The University of California Extension,
Berkeley, California

# CLEAR TECHNICAL WRITING

McGRAW-HILL BOOK COMPANY

NEW YORK
ST. LOUIS
SAN FRANCISCO
DÜSSELDORF
JOHANNESBURG
KUALA LUMPUR
LONDON
MEXICO
MONTREAL
NEW DELHI
PANAMA
RIO DE JANEIRO
SINGAPORE
SYDNEY
TORONTO

Library of Congress Cataloging in Publication Data

Brogan, John A.
   Clear technical writing.

   1. Technical writing.   I. Title.

T11.B68      808'.066'6021      72-13702
ISBN 0-07-007974-9

**Clear Technical Writing**

67890EBEB   798

Design: Marsha Cohen

*To my father
and in memory of my mother*

# CONTENTS

# PREFACE

This book can help you develop a writing style that is direct, clear, and concise. Already, in its development stages, it has done that for employees in industry and government and for many students. The text will involve you continuously with short, easy, learning steps. After a few hours—the entire book does not require more than sixteen—you will find yourself eliminating writing impediments (gobbledygook) from your writing.

The book's effectiveness grew out of extensive research and testing which led to subsequent revisions. Among its outstanding features are:

○ Self-teaching—letting you work independently at your own speed.
○ Practical—attacking the most common writing faults.
○ Efficient—saving you hours over conventional texts.

## The Need

People in technical fields need to express their ideas clearly. Engineers spend 50 to 70 percent of their time communicating; their supervisors, even more; technicians, scientists, and other technologists, often as much. The rewards are high for those who can communicate effectively—in professional recognition, advancement, self-satisfaction, and salary. One estimate is that an engineer can earn up to $120,000 more in his lifetime if he is an effective writer. Yet the President's Science Advisory Committee felt it necessary to express its concern: "That so many American scientists and technologists can neither write nor speak effective English; that the new language of science and technology is turgid, heavy, and unclear."

## The Content—Removing Noise Sources

The subject matter of this book is the result of extensive analysis of unclear sentences written by scores of engineers, scientists, technicians, and their supervisors. (Many of these sentences appear in this book as problem sentences.) The study showed the major sources of unclarity to be the following: redundancies, weak verbs, abstract nouns, showy writing, improper subordination, misused passives, "it's" and "there's," commas, hyphens, and styles that were either overly impersonal or falsely personal. For more detail, glance at the table of contents. It is with these and related matters that this book deals.

The faults I mentioned hinder the effectiveness of communications by giving unnecessary and misleading information. In communications theory, superfluous information is called "noise"; these sources of unclarity are "noise" sources. They are "semantic noise" sources—a noise of meanings (to be distinguished from "engineering noise," such as static and transient waves from equipment and the medium). Though it overloads their sentences, and burdens and misguides their readers, most writers do not know they are creating semantic noise. The major purpose of this text is to help you become aware of noise sources. For example, you will learn to remove simple repetitions of meaning, such as "We are *actively* testing"; overly heavy words, such as "It *exists,*" rather than "It *is*"; and ponderous expressions: "We *made a measurement,*" when "We *measured*" would do.

## The Method—Programmed Learning

This text uses a proven method that has grown out of the techniques of programmed learning. A short text explains a source of semantic noise. You immediately apply this knowledge to problem sentences having similar noise sources. This allows one to immediately apply learned material. Alongside each problem sentence is a box containing the correct response. You are to check here immediately after making your response. Instantaneous checking reinforces your correct answers, and prevents erroneous responses from becoming fixed. Frequent reviews heighten the reinforcement. Comments interspersed between the frames give exceptions to and modifications of the rules. Hints and clues help with difficult sentences.

The text develops in a tight logical order that excludes irrelevant matter. This logical development and the emphasis on eliminating unnecessary information makes it possible to bypass most of the conceptual apparatus of traditional grammar. The basic grammar that is necessary—such as identifying subjects and verbs—is taught when needed, usually inductively.

The self-teaching nature of this text allows students to work at their own pace, either independently of a class or as assigned by an instructor. This frees instructors for personal consultations and for class discussion and analysis. Instructors can monitor student progress with tests available with the instructor manual.

Those who are familiar with the books of Robert Gunning and Rudolf Flesch will recognize my debts to them. I wish to express my gratitude to Russell L. Heiserman, Director of Research for Hickok Teaching Systems, Inc. for his kind help in bringing this text to publication. Also, without the many helpful comments of my students, this text would never have attained its present effectiveness.

*John A. Brogan*

## HOW TO USE THIS BOOK

Understand the text fully before going to the frames. Especially, be sure you can make changes like those in the example sentences. You will be called upon to make similar changes in problem sentences.

Here is a diagram of a frame:

---

*INSTRUCTION BOX*

---

Clue

Correct response                                 Problem sentence

---

You are to cover the left half of the frame (the clue and the correct response) while revising the problem sentence as directed by the instruction box. When you finish, look at the correct response and compare it with yours.

Often, as above, the left half has two levels. Check the clue in the upper level only after trying your best to do as instructed. The clue will let you know if you are on the right track. Or if you run into difficulty in carrying out the instruction, the clue can put you right. When you have revised the sentence to your satisfaction in the light of the clue, check your version against the correct response. While doing this, quickly review the change made in the problem sentence.

### Some Words of Caution

○ Never check the left side—neither the clue nor the correct response—until after you have applied yourself seriously to correcting the sentence. Checking left too soon will cheat you of the analysis these frames foster. If necessary, you can always restudy the example sentence.

○ You should always make full responses. Write out words where called for, especially where their endings change. Obvious abbreviations can sometimes be used.

○ Check the left side immediately after you make your response. Delaying a few seconds can destroy the effect of this quick feedback, which is integral to the form of teaching used in this book.

○ A few seconds' reviewing of what you have done while checking the correct response will immensely reinforce the lesson. Do it while your attempt is fresh in your mind.

○ To aid with later reviews, mark frames in which you have difficulty with a large X on the line separating the problem sentence from the clue and correct response. For a review, you can quickly reread the text and then concentrate on the marked frames.

○ Understandably, you will disagree with some revisions. But even when disagreeing, try to understand the principle behind suggested changes.

# CLEAR
# TECHNICAL
# WRITING

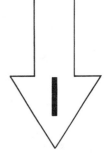

# REMOVING REDUNDANCIES

Use all the words you need to get your message across, but no more. Especially be wary of redundancies, needless repetitions of meaning, as in "It was red in color," where "in color" unnecessarily repeats a meaning carried by "red." The repetition suggests that "red" is used elsewhere with a meaning other than that of color—"Red alerts were sounded on sirens." Such misleading suggestions misdirect attention and obscure your message.

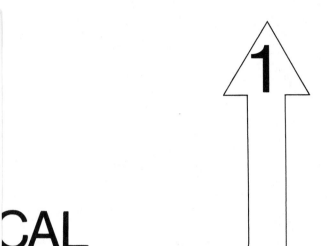

CAL

**"Period Of"**

...ne, as in:

...utes for checking the incoming lines.

...ely repeats a meaning carried by "ten minutes."

...utes for checking the incoming lines.

(Use a circle and the delete symbol — ℓ— for deletions.)

Two expressions (words or phrases) are underlined in the following example sentence. One is unnecessary. Delete it before you read on.

**The solution is first stirred <u>and then</u> heated.**

The unnecessary word is "and"; "then" carries its meaning.

**The solution is first stirred, ⟨and⟩then heated.**

Note that removing "then" would have changed the meaning: it would have taken out the notion of sequence in time. (A comma is inserted where "and" is understood—that is, not expressed.)

Again, before you read beyond the following sentence, decide which of the underlined expressions is superfluous; then delete it.

**Their identification numbers <u>are not known</u> <u>at this time</u>.**

You should have deleted "at this time"; it is not necessary, since "are not known" means at this time — now.

**Their identification numbers are not known.**

○ Place your left hand over the left half of the frames below.
○ The problem sentence in the right half has two underlined time expressions. Delete the unnecessary expression in the first frame. Do it now.
○ Then take away your left hand to check your deletion against the correct response given there.
○ Quickly review what you have done before going to the next frame.

| | |
|---|---|
| You should have deleted:<br>(time of) | The computer executes instructions during the remaining <u>time of</u> 20 milliseconds. |
| You should have deleted:<br>(during the period) | This report describes work done <u>during the period</u> from March 1965 to March 1966. |
| (a time interval of) | After <u>a time interval of</u> <u>one-half to two minutes</u>, the speaker tone usually stops. |
| (from time to time) | Call a conference <u>from time to time</u> <u>when necessary</u>. (Remove the less specific expression.) |
| the space of | With proper planning we can prepare high-quality proposals in <u>the space of</u> a few weeks. |
| a duration of | This set operated for <u>a duration of</u> <u>ten hours</u>. |
| given | Only one tape unit operates at a <u>given</u> time. |
| , and | The output of this filter is amplified <u>and</u> <u>then</u> filtered. |

The remaining frames are generally like those below: not all the sentences have underlines, and the left half has two levels. The upper levels give clues — two expressions, one of which is to be deleted. Look at them only after you have made your correction and want to be sure you are on the right track or if, after diligent effort, you still have difficulty. The lower level gives the correct response. Check there only after you have fully revised the problem sentence.

| | |
|---|---|
| You should have deleted one of<br>the following:<br>During / periods of<br>(periods of) | During <u>periods of</u> unusually hot weather the reserve air conditioner aids the main one. |
| time / interval<br>(interval) | The amplitude is proportional to the <u>time interval</u> between zero crossings. |

| | |
|---|---|
| ten hours / in duration<br>(in duration) ✓ | The timer measures intervals of up to <u>ten</u> <u>hours</u> in <u>duration</u>. |

COMMENT: WHENEVER YOU DELETE THE WRONG WORD, TRY BEFORE GOING ON TO THE NEXT FRAME TO UNDERSTAND WHERE YOU WENT WRONG. YOU WILL USUALLY FIND THAT THE SUPERFLUOUS WORD HAS A MEANING ANOTHER WORD ALSO CARRIES. IN THE PRECEDING FRAME, FOR EXAMPLE, THE MEANING OF THE SUPERFLUOUS "DURATION" WAS PRESENT IN "TEN HOURS."

| | |
|---|---|
| and / then<br>ʌ(and) ✓ | This signal is amplified and then detected and filtered. |
| in the future / can be made<br>(in the future) ✓ | We will design these devices so that in the future they can be made of solid-state silicon. |
| indicated / in advance<br>(in advance) ✓ | The analysis before simulation indicated in advance how the system would operate. |

## 1-2  Quantity Words: "A Total Of," "Range Of," "Amount Of"

Technical writing abounds in references to quantity. And, as might be expected, many of these references are unnecessary. Among them are phrases like "a total of" and "the amount of" when used with precise totals or amounts:

We burned out (a total of) twelve lamps.

"Twelve" specifies the total.

*DELETE UNNECESSARY QUANTITY WORDS*

| | |
|---|---|
| a total of / thirty-six switches<br>(a total of) ✓ | The front panel contains a total of thirty-six switches. |
| The extent of / is wide<br>(The extent of) ✓ | The extent of his experience is wide. |
| density / figure<br>(figure) ✓ | We will try to reduce the <u>density</u> <u>figure</u>. |
| sufficient / quantity of<br>(quantity of) ✓ | He will still have <u>sufficient</u> <u>quantity of</u> attitude-control gas. |

COMMENT: IN YOUR REVIEW OF WHAT YOU HAVE DONE IN EACH FRAME, NOTE HOW THE SUPERFLUOUS EXPRESSION DISTRACTS FROM MORE IMPORTANT WORDS.

| | |
|---|---|
| a rate of / 10 angstroms per second<br>~~a rate of~~ ✓ | The films grew at a rate of 10 angstroms per second. |
| at a point / 3 decibels below<br>~~at a point~~ ✓ | Demodulation continues even when the R-F signal is at a point 3 decibels below the apparent receiver threshold. |
| amount of / reflection<br>~~amount of~~ ✓ | The <u>amount of</u> <u>reflection</u> will be excessive unless the characteristics of the printed conductors match those of the line. |
| the range of / the . . . dc range<br>~~the range of~~ ✓ | Switch the range of the meter to the 0- to 50-volt dc range. |

COMMENT: THE PRECEDING SENTENCE CAN ALSO BE REWRITTEN: "SWITCH THE RANGE OF THE METER TO 0 TO 50 VOLTS DC."

| | |
|---|---|
| noise / level<br>~~level~~ ✓ | To reduce the noise level we coated the hood with sound-deadening material. |
| amount of / equipment<br>~~amount of~~ ✓ | The modular design reduces the amount of equipment that must be kept in the warehouse. |
| the value of / the bias current<br>~~the value of~~ ✓ | Adjust the value of the bias current for optimum detector sensitivity. |
| a minimum of / 1000<br>~~a minimum of~~ ✓ | The temperature ranged from a minimum of 1000 to 1800°C. |
| the composition of / 50 to 100 percent.<br>~~the composition of~~ ✓ | The composition of the film is 50 to 100 percent zinc sulfide. |
| the temperature of / 1300 and 1400°C<br>~~the temperature of~~ ✓ | The temperature of this cup was kept between 1300 and 1400°C. |

COMMENT: NOTE THAT YOU HAVE BEEN SHORTENING SOME SENTENCES BY UP TO ONE-THIRD THEIR ORIGINAL LENGTH. NOT ONLY DOES THE PADDING YOU HAVE REMOVED WASTE READER'S TIME, BUT, MORE IMPORTANT, IT DULLS THE MESSAGE'S IMPACT. LEAN WRITING THRUSTS THE ESSENTIAL IDEAS VIGOROUSLY FORWARD.

## 1-3 Dimension Words: "In Size," "In Direction"

The redundancies in the following problem sentences are similar to the preceding ones. Try removing them from the following:

**The new beam is smaller in size.**

**Turn the knob in a clockwise direction.**

If you are unsure, reread the sentences, leaving out words that might be unnecessary. Your revisions should have been:

**The new beam is smaller ~~in size.~~**

**Turn the knob ~~in a~~ clockwise ~~direction.~~**

## DELETE DEAD DIMENSION WORDS

| | |
|---|---|
| in the direction / to communicate<br>~~in the direction~~ | The 10-foot antennas can be turned in the direction to communicate with transportable stations. |
| 6 by 6 feet / in size<br>~~in size~~ | The display is 6 by 6 feet in size. |
| physically / in<br>~~physically~~ | The power generator is not physically in the building. |
| clockwise / in a . . . direction<br>~~in a . . . direction~~ | Turn the knob in a clockwise direction. |
| parabolic / in shape<br>~~in shape~~ | The reflectors are parabolic in shape. |

## 1-4   Activity Words: "Work," "Function," "Action"

Words like "test," "boiling," and "study" describe specific activities yet often have vague activity words written with them, as in the following sentences:

**The boiling ~~action~~ continued.**

**Finish the cost analysis ~~effort~~ before you submit the proposal.**

## DELETE UNNECESSARY ACTIVITY WORDS

| | |
|---|---|
| search / function<br>~~function~~ | The search function can be performed rapidly. |
| simulation / effort<br>~~effort~~ | The simulation effort tested intelligibility and voice quality. |
| operation / faster<br>~~In operation~~ | In operation our computer is faster. |

| | |
|---|---|
| evaporation / the . . . technique<br>(the) . . . (technique) | We will use the vacuum evaporation technique. |

COMMENT: AT THE UPPER LEFT OF THE PRECEDING FRAME ALL WORDS IN THE EXPRESSION TO BE DELETED WERE GIVEN: "THE" AND "TECHNIQUE." MOST OF THE REMAINING FRAMES GIVE ONLY THE IMPORTANT WORD, LEAVING OUT WORDS LIKE "THE" AND "OF." TO BE SURE YOU REMOVE ALL UNNECESSARY WORDS, REREAD THE SENTENCES BEFORE CHECKING LEFT.

| | |
|---|---|
| extraction / process<br>(process) for (the) . . . (process) | This new device simplifies the extraction process. |
| survey / action<br>(action) | We can begin the site survey action immediately. |
| training / function<br>(function) | Mr. David Jordan directs the training function. |
| work / studies<br>(work in) | We have been supporting work in basic speech studies for many years. |
| modulation / applications<br>(applications) | In cross modulation applications, field reversal does not increase frequency. |
| test / procedure<br>(procedure) | Remove all channels from service during the test procedure. |
| fuel / purposes<br>(purposes) | It is used for fuel purposes. |

## 1-5   Object Words: "Equipment," "Unit," "Facility"

Words like "equipment," "unit," and "device" are superfluous when used with words that adequately identify the item, as in:

Turn on the transmitter receiver (unit.)

The name of the unit is the "transmitter receiver."
    You will have to rewrite some names slightly, as in:

The coils are invaluable in frequency-limiting devices.

This becomes:

The coils are invaluable in frequency limiters.

By similar changes "transmit*ting* equipment" becomes "transmit*ters*." "Heat*ing* equipment" becomes "heat*ers*." "Permut*ing* devices" (encoders and decoders) becomes "permut*ers*." These are natural changes which you will find easy to make.

## DELETE SUPERFLUOUS OBJECT WORDS

| | |
|---|---|
| processor / unit <br> (unit) | The central processor unit manipulates data in the core memory. |
| transportation / facilities <br> (facilities) | Their army cannot furnish transportation facilities for our engineers. |
| radio / equipment <br> (equipment) | This section explains how to apply power to the radio equipment. |

You will have to rewrite the following sentences slightly:

| | |
|---|---|
| communications-control / device <br> (device) (a communications con-trol*ler*) | The input-output processor is a communications-control device. |
| component / assemblies <br> (assemblies) (component*s*.) | The frame is also a base for mounting the other component assemblies. |
| camera / equipment <br> (equipment) (*transmitters* and *cameras*.) | We have also manufactured TV transmitting and camera equipment. |
| latching / mechanism <br> The *latch*ing (mechanism) | The latching mechanism had broken. |
| mail-handling/unit <br> (unit) (mail hand*ler*) | We ran a deck of mixed mail through the mail-handling unit. |

COMMENT: TAKE CARE THAT IN MAKING CHANGES LIKE THE PRECEDING YOU DO NOT BRING ON OTHER FAULTS. "MAIL HANDLER," FOR EXAMPLE, MIGHT MEAN A PERSON AS WELL AS A MACHINE. IF A DELETION MIGHT LEAD TO AMBIGUITY, AS IN A CONTEXT WHERE BOTH PERSONS AND MACHINES ARE CALLED MAIL HANDLERS, DON'T MAKE THE DELETION. PUT CLARITY FIRST.

## 1-6 Review

Remove superfluous expressions from the following sentences. Continue reviewing what you have done before you leave each frame.

| | |
|---|---|
| emitter / unit <br> (unit) | The impedance to ground of the emitter unit increased. |

| | |
|---|---|
| total / seven fonts<br>(a total of) | The test deck contained a total of the seven fonts listed below. |
| speed / characters per second<br>(at a speed of) | The paper-tape punch and reader can punch and read at a speed of fifty characters per second. |
| central switching / facility<br>(facility) (a central switch.) | The control section acts as a central switching facility. (Revise slightly.) |
| test / procedure<br>(procedure) | A diagnostic program carries out this test procedure. |
| engineering / effort<br>(the) (effort) | List the hours each man spent on the value engineering effort. |

COMMENT: IN FRAMES LIKE THE ABOVE, THE PARENTHESES MEAN AN OPTIONAL DELETION.

| | |
|---|---|
| period / eight weeks<br>(a period of) | The civil-engineering survey will last a period of eight weeks. |
| physically / smaller<br>(physically) | Physically it is smaller than either of the others. |
| transmission / purposes<br>(purposes) (or: When transmitting) | For transmission purposes have the needle on green. |
| completed / work on<br>(work on) | Our company has completed work on several arch dams. |
| amount / the loss<br>(The amount of) | The amount of the loss was less than expected. |
| directions / perpendicular<br>(in directions) (perpendicular*ly*) | The two beams are polarized in directions perpendicular to each other. ("Perpendicular" becomes perpendicular*ly*.) |
| limiting / devices<br>(devices) (are noise limit*ers*) | Tunnel-diode amplifiers are noise-limiting devices. (Rewrite slightly.) |
| uniform / at a . . . rate<br>(at a) . . . (rate) (spent *uni-<br>formly*) | The research money will be spent at a uniform rate over the year. ("Uniform" becomes "uniformly.") |
| modulation / equipment<br>(equipment) (phase modula*tors*) | We have designed phase-modulation equipment for testing these diodes. (Rewrite slightly.) |

COMMENT: WHEN AN EXPRESSION LIKE "PHASE-MODULATION EQUIPMENT" MEANS THE PHASE MODULATOR AND OTHER EQUIPMENT, SAY THAT:

We have designed phase modulators, *their test sets, and* . . .

OR

. . . phase modulators and associated equipment.

| | |
|---|---|
| range / from 4,400 to 5,000 mega-hertz <br> ~~In the range of~~ | In the range of from 4,400 to 5,000 mega-hertz the termination load dissipates 1,000 watts. |
| search / operation <br> ~~operation~~ | The tape-search operation oscillates the tape forward and backward. |
| two / (2) <br> ~~(2)~~ | Only two (2) inspectors have been assigned to the other branches. |

COMMENT: THE REPETITION OF NUMBERS AS FIGURES IN PARENTHESES HAS NOT BEEN NEEDED SINCE TYPEWRITERS REPLACED HANDWRITING.

| | |
|---|---|
| and / then <br> ~~and~~ (; then) | This proposal develops these specifications, presenting first the possibilities and then the suggested approach. |
| position / center <br> ~~a position at~~ | The image is scanned outward from a position at the center. |
| taken / past <br> ~~in the past~~ | Similar projects in the past have taken us to many lands. |
| smaller / size <br> ~~in size~~ | The new switch is smaller in size. |
| excitation / function <br> ~~the~~ ~~function~~ | This will cut the percentage of the bit rate needed for the hybrid excitation function. |
| pumping / assembly <br> The fluid pump~~ing assembly~~ | The fluid pumping assembly consists of two semi-independent systems. (Rewrite slightly.) |
| level / −20 dbm <br> ~~a level of~~ | The meter will then show a level of −20 dbm. |
| a minimum of / 100°C; a maxi-mum of / 120°C <br> ~~a minimum of;~~ ~~a maximum of~~ | The temperature ranged from a minimum of 100°C to a maximum of 120°C. (Two changes are needed.) |

| | |
|---|---|
| degree / improvement <br> ~~degree of~~ | These plots show the degree of improvement from efficient analysis. |
| two / both <br> ~~both~~ | The two transmitters are both alike in the following ways. |

COMMENT: THE WORD "EQUIPMENT" SHOULD NOT BE DELETED FROM A SENTENCE LIKE THE FOLLOWING:

All transmitting and receiving *equipment* except the power amplifiers are in one van.

HERE "EQUIPMENT" HELPS DISTINGUISH BETWEEN TWO TYPES OF TRANSMITTING AND RECEIVING EQUIPMENT.

# MOSTLY NONTECHNICAL WORDS

The deadwood in the following sentences consist for the most part of nontechnical expressions.

### 2-1 "Type" Words: "Type," "Nature," and "Condition"

Words like "type," "nature," and "condition" are often needless jargon:

The coil is mounted on a hinged (type) panel.

The book was (of a) technical (nature.)

---

*DELETE DEADWOOD*

---

| | |
|---|---|
| type of / calibrator<br>(type of) | We replaced it with a simple, reliable, inexpensive type of calibrator. |
| short / in nature<br>(in nature) | The motions are short in nature. |
| area / analysis<br>(the area of) | He has been working in the area of reliability analysis. |

---

COMMENT: NOTE AS YOU REVIEW EACH FRAME HOW THE DEADWOOD DETRACT FROM THE IMPORTANT WORDS. IN THE PRECEDING FRAME, FOR EXAMPLE, "THE AREA OF" UNDERCUTS "RELIABILITY ANALYSIS."

| | |
|---|---|
| green / condition<br>(the) . . . (condition) | The light changes to the green condition. |
| mechanical / nature<br>electrical / nature<br>(of a) . . . (nature)<br>(of an) . . . (nature) | The problem seems to be more of a mechanical nature than of an electrical nature. (Two changes are needed.) |
| delay / feature<br>(feature) | This alarm has a built-in delay feature. |
| emitter / one<br>(the one) | The thermionic emitter is the one best suited to develop such a beam. |
| reliability / factor<br>(a) . . . (factor) | This design has a high reliability factor. |
| cost / factor<br>(factor) | The cost factor may be prohibitive. |
| as-required / basis<br>(on an) as required (basis) (no hyphen) | They participate on an as-required basis. |
| off-line / capacity<br>(in an) . . . (capacity) | The processor operates mainly in an off-line capacity. |

You will have to rewrite some of the following sentences slightly:

| | |
|---|---|
| problem / areas<br>(areas) (problems) | The first run on 14,000 pieces of mail revealed no significant problem areas. |
| schematic / form<br>(in) . . . (form) (schematically) | The read-write-select circuit appears in schematic form in Figure 7. ("Schematic" becomes "schematically.") |
| similar / in . . . fashion<br>(in) . . . (fashion) (Similarly,) | In similar fashion, an electron that starts out in direction KB turns onto path KDP. ("Similar" becomes "similarly.") |
| Alphabetical / order<br>(into) . . . (order) (alphabetically) | Sort items for the author list into alphabetical order. ("Alphabetical" becomes "alphabetically.") |
| similar / manner<br>(in a) . . . (manner) (similarly) | It regulates variations in the load voltage in a similar manner. |
| different / from a . . . angle<br>(from a) . . . (angle) (differently) | We approached the data from a different angle. |

| | |
|---|---|
| on an . . . basis / as-required <br> ~~on an~~ . . ~~basis~~ (as required) | A technical advisory group is available to the project manager on an as-required basis. |
| in an . . . manner / identical <br> ~~in an~~ . . . ~~manner~~ (identica*lly*) | The other segments operate in an identical manner. |
| rapid / sequence <br> ~~in~~ . . ~~sequence~~ (rapid*ly*) | This could occur if the flow were turned off and on in rapid sequence. |

COMMENT: "TYPE" MIGHT BE PROPERLY USED IN A SENTENCE LIKE THE FOLLOWING:

The army can provide a *DC-10–type* aircraft.

ITS USE IS FITTING IF A DC-10 *OR A PLANE LIKE IT* IS TO BE PROVIDED. IT IS INCORRECT IF NOTHING BUT A DC-10 WILL BE PROVIDED. IN THAT CASE, "TYPE" IS NOT ONLY SUPERFLUOUS BUT ALSO MISLEADING.

## 2-2  Attention Getters: "In Order," "In Fact," "In Case"

Some expressions merely inform readers that something is going to be said. They are as unnecessary as are the throat clearings, "uh-uhs," and "harrumphs" many speakers use for the same purpose. Among such throat clearers are "in order," as in:

~~In order~~ to start the motor, push the red button.

"In order" means "for the purpose of," but so does "to" in "to start." In the following sentence "the results of" is not necessary:

~~The results of~~ our calculations support his theories.

### DELETE DEADWOOD

| | |
|---|---|
| in order / to keep <br> ~~in order~~ | Diode CR4 was added in order to keep the input signal from exceeding the $V_{beo}$ of Q14. |
| fact / shift does not <br> ~~the fact~~ | However, keep in mind the fact that the phase shift does not of itself distort the output speed. |

COMMENT: AS YOU REVIEW EACH FRAME, NOTICE HOW LITTLE CONTENT THE ELIMINATED EXPRESSION CARRIES—JUST ENOUGH TO DISTRACT ATTENTION.

| | |
|---|---|
| results / estimate <br> ~~The results of~~ | Compare the results of this estimate of reliability with the reliability required by our contract. |

| | |
|---|---|
| case / electrolytes<br>(the) case of | For the case of alkaline electrolytes we need adequate corrosion inhibitors. |
| clarification / purposes<br>(purposes of) | For purposes of definition and clarification let us divide the project-management organization into two areas. |
| nature / curve<br>(The nature of) | The nature of the frequency-response curve can be changed by changing the intensity of the light source. |
| reason / difference<br>(The reason for) | The reason for this difference can be attributed to the asynchronous operation of the computer. |
| fact / completing<br>(the fact) | Another important consideration is the fact that our department is completing two projects nearby. |
| point / new . . . must be bought<br>(the point) | Our earlier report stressed the point that new equipment must be bought. |
| possibility / galvanic action<br>(the possibility of) | To prevent the possibility of galvanic action between dissimilar metals, all metal parts are of copper. |
| cases / where . . . states occur.<br>(in cases) | High temperatures are especially necessary in cases where metastable states occur. |
| In all cases / where . . . is used<br>(In all cases) | In all cases where scatter transmission was necessary, we used 10- and 15-foot antennas. |
| order / avoid<br>(In order) | In order to avoid chemical interactions, deposit the second layer in a vacuum. |

COMMENT: "IN ORDER" IS ALMOST ALWAYS DEADWOOD AT THE BEGINNING OF A SENTENCE. ELSEWHERE, IT USUALLY IS —BUT NOT ALWAYS. IN THE FOLLOWING SENTENCE, FOR EXAMPLE, "IN ORDER" PREVENTS AN AMBIGUOUS READING:

This value was made a variable *in order* to find the optimum value. (That is, for the purpose of finding the . . .)

IF "IN ORDER" IS TAKEN OUT, THE SENTENCE CAN BE UNDERSTOOD AS SUGGESTING NOT ONLY "FOR THE PURPOSE OF FINDING" BUT ALSO THAT THE VARIABLE VALUE FINDS THE OPTIMUM VALUE.

## 2-3 Actuality Words: "Actual," "Active," "Existing"

Words like "actual" and "existing" are superfluous when they do not draw a contrast between the actual and the nonactual, the existent and the nonexistent. For example, unless the following sentence is in a context that contrasts existing equipment with nonexisting (planned, proposed, discarded) equipment, "existing" is not necessary:

Our ~~existing~~ strain gauge is worthless for this test.

Similarly for "the presence of" in:

The computer printout discloses ~~the presence of~~ coding errors.

## DELETE DEAD EXISTENCE WORDS

| | |
|---|---|
| presence / detects . . . targets<br>~~the presence of~~ | The primary radar detects the presence of moving targets. |
| actively / studying the<br>~~actively~~ | Our company has been actively studying the practicability of metal-air batteries. |
| actually / installed<br>~~actually~~ | The facilities engineering department actually installed the navigation aids. |
| actual / design of<br>~~actual~~ | Our department will finish actual design of the prototype this week. |
| actually / changes<br>~~actually~~ | It reverses if the polarity of the input actually changes. |
| existing / schedules<br>~~existing~~ | Are the existing schedules accurate? |
| actively / is providing<br>~~actively~~ | This department is actively providing technical services to many government agencies. |
| presence / paper in<br>~~The presence of~~ | The presence of a sheet of paper in the transport interrupts the flow. |
| real and active / saving<br>~~real and active~~ | We can convert these exchanges of antenna size and radiation-hop distance into real and active dollar savings. |

COMMENT: READABILITY STUDIES CONFIRM—WHAT MOST PEOPLE KNOW—THAT LONG SENTENCES ARE HARDER TO UNDERSTAND THAN SHORTER ONES. REMOVING DEADWOOD INCREASES READABILITY, SINCE IT SHORTENS SENTENCES.

## 2-4 Propriety Words: "Proper," "Suitable," "Appropriate"

Much deadwood results from calling something proper, appropriate, or fitting, when the propriety, appropriateness, or fittingness can be taken for granted. A lady *is* "proper"; she need not be called a "proper lady." In a similar way, "properly" is not needed in sentences like the following:

To (properly) align the receiver do the following.

Instructions, like any other human product, might be faulty, but the writer's good intentions can be taken for granted.

## *DELETE PROPRIETY DEADWOOD*

| | |
|---|---|
| necessary / needed<br>(necessary) | The 70-MC amplifier gives the <u>necessary</u> gain and selectivity <u>needed</u> for each channel. |
| align / properly<br>(properly) | Now that we have solved these problems, we can properly align the channels. |
| suitably / treated<br>(suitably) | The electrodes are a porous nickle mesh <u>suitably</u> <u>treated</u> to maximize the reaction. |
| associated / text<br>(associated) | The drawings support the associated text. |
| own / particular<br>(particular) | This signal produces a tape that has its own particular routing. |
| correct / identification<br>(correct) | Correct identification cannot be made. |
| appropriate / error code<br>(appropriate) | Before it stops, the program prints out the appropriate error code. |
| available / facilities<br>(available) | Designs for boards larger than 16 by 16 inches will not be accepted, because available photographic facilities in our plant cannot handle larger boards. |

COMMENT: IN THE PRECEDING FRAME, "AVAILABLE" SUGGESTS THAT THOUGH THERE ARE FACILITIES FOR LARGER BOARDS, THESE FACILITIES CANNOT BE USED.

| | |
|---|---|
| its / associated<br>(associated) | Their department designed Sideswiper and its associated control system. |
| their / respective<br>(respective) | It plotted the timing points at the center of their respective intervals. |

COMMENT: WORDS LIKE "PROPER" AND "CORRECT" CAN OFTEN BE REPLACED BY MORE PRECISE STATEMENTS. A SENTENCE LIKE "DETECTION REDUCES THE THRESHOLD LEVEL *PROPERLY*" SHOULD PROBABLY BE REWRITTEN WITH SOME MORE EXACT PHRASE, SUCH AS ". . . REDUCES . . . AT THE PROPER RATE," ". . . AT THE RATE OF 3 DECIBELS FOR EACH . . . ," OR ". . . AT THE RIGHT TIME."

## 2-5 Emphasis Words: "Any," "All," "Some"

Some words add little more than emphasis or intensity, for example, "very" in:

A *very* precise chronometer.

A statement of the precision would be better:

A chronometer precise to the ten-thousandth of a second a day.

Otherwise, since there is little meaningful difference between "precise" and "very precise," words like "very" can usually be removed:

A precise chronometer.

Similarly "all" can often be taken for granted in sentences like:

Inspect all the braces on the damaged side.

"Inspect the braces" means inspect them all.

## DELETE DEAD EMPHASIS WORDS

| | |
|---|---|
| any / . . . covers; any / . . . lamps <br> any   any | Remove any cracked indicator covers and any burned-out indicator lamps. (Delete two.) |
| some / value <br> some | When fully developed, it will have some value in speech analysis. |
| a great / many <br> a great | The circuit that follows must have a great many diodes. |
| overall / system growth <br> overall | This design allows for overall system growth. |
| all / the air <br> all | It must have enough area to pass all the air for the heat exchanger. |
| highly / useful <br> highly | This device is highly useful in speech analysis. |

| | |
|---|---|
| very / acceptable<br>(very) | Either specimen would be very acceptable. |
| any / grease or oil<br>(any) | Remove any grease or oil with solvent and a soft cloth. |

COMMENT: SHORT SIMPLE WORDS LIKE "ANY" AND "ALL" CERTAINLY DO NOT LENGTHEN SENTENCES MUCH. SO OBJECTING TO THEM MAY SEEM FOOLISH, AND IF LENGTH WERE THE ONLY OBJECTION, IT MIGHT BE. HOWEVER, AS WITH MOST OTHER SUPERFLUOUS WORDS, THE SERIOUS DANGER OF THESE WORDS IS THAT THEY ARE MISLEADING. THE DIRECTION TO "CHECK *ALL* THE BRACES ON THE DAMAGED SIDE" SUGGESTS THAT ELSEWHERE OTHER BRACES ARE DEALT WITH, POSSIBLY:

Check *the horizontal* braces for the following defects: . . . Check *the vertical* braces for. . . .

## 2-6 Review

### DELETE DEADWOOD

| | |
|---|---|
| fact / the metals are similar<br>(the fact) | Extensive tests confirmed the fact that the two metals are similar. |
| order / ensure<br>(in order) | This is necessary in order to ensure symmetrical limiting in the received signal. |
| results / studies<br>(the results of) | The results of earlier studies led to a mathematical model of a wheel in motion. |
| case / lists are needed<br>(in the case) | This is true only in the case where two or more lists are needed. |
| nature of / construction<br>(The) nature of | The nature of program construction for this computer is unique. |
| fact / losses become<br>(the fact) | The drawback is the fact that the losses soon become prohibitive. |
| capacity / head<br>(In his capacity) | In his capacity as head of the alphanumeric group he worked on recognition of constrained hand printing. |
| possibility / error<br>(the possibility of) | To reduce the possibility of errors, their engineers installed an error-detection circuit. |
| order / determine<br>(in order) | Some I-V measurements will be made in order to learn if X varies with temperature. |

COMMENT: DELETING "IN ORDER" FROM THE FOLLOWING SENTENCE MAKES IT AMBIGUOUS:

We rejected their device (in order) to maintain the compatability of the system despite future changes.

**THIS CAN BE UNDERSTOOD AS SAYING:**

We rejected *their device that maintains* the compatibility. . . .

**BUT THE ORIGINAL SENTENCE HAD AN ENTIRELY DIFFERENT MESSAGE:**

We rejected their device *so that we can maintain* compatibility. . . ."

**AND PROBABLY THAT IS THE BEST WAY TO WRITE IT.**

| | |
|---|---|
| automatic / basis <br> (on a) . . (basis) (continuous*ly* and automatic*ally.*) | This circuit checks the operability of the computer on a <u>continuous and automatic basis</u>. (Rewrite slightly.) |
| any / dust <br> (any) | Remove any dust or other foreign material from the case. |
| cordless / of the . . . type <br> (of the) . . (type) | These motors are of the cordless type. |
| assembled / condition <br> (in a) . . (condition) | The transit was shipped in a fully assembled condition. |

COMMENT: "CONDITION" IS NECESSARY IN SENTENCES LIKE "WIRES FROM THE MAINTENANCE CONSOLE DRIVE THE LINE-CONDITION INDICATORS": THE INDICATORS SHOW THE CONDITION OF THE LINE, POSSIBLY INDICATING WHETHER OR NOT THE LINE IS OPERATING AND CAN CARRY A FULL LOAD.

| | |
|---|---|
| serial / in . . . form <br> (in) . . (form) (seria*lly*.) | It would be hard to load the addresses in <u>serial form</u>. (Rewrite slightly.) |
| correctly / identified <br> (correctly) | Electronic parts are correctly identified by reference-designation numbers. |
| areas / where <br> (in those areas) | You can keep the old housings <u>in those areas where</u> they are compatible with the new. |
| reason / one <br> (one of) | The reason was one of simplicity and low cost. |
| instantaneous / basis <br> (on an) . . (basis) (instantane*ously*) | It controlled the deposition rate on an instantaneous basis. |

COMMENT: IN SENTENCES LIKE THE PRECEDING YOU ARE CHANGING ADJECTIVES (IN NOUN PHRASES) INTO ADVERBS: "INSTANTANEOUS" TO "INSTANTANEOUSLY." (THE "-LY" ENDING USUALLY MEANS A WORD IS AN ADVERB.) NOTE HOW MUCH MORE SMOOTHLY THESE SENTENCES READ WITH ADVERBS IN PLACE OF NOUN PHRASES.

| | |
|---|---|
| suitable / manner<br>(in a) . . . (manner) (suitably) | This flexible link conforms to the specifications and performs in a suitable manner. |
| order / make<br>(in order) | These operations have been simplified purposely in order to make the lift more practical. |
| limiting / factor<br>(a) . . . (factor) | The electronic components are a size-limiting factor only in the smallest modules. |
| presence / requires . . . field<br>(the presence of) | Optical pumping requires the presence of a small, homogeneous magnetic field. |
| actively / will participate<br>(actively) | Our engineers will participate actively in this research. |
| present / found . . . on<br>(to be present) | After some operations, free indium was found to be present on the deposited films. |
| some / value<br>(some) | Many speech parameters have some value in speech recognition. |
| properly / make<br>(properly) | To properly make this check, overlap the data one clock pulse. |
| can be commanded / case<br>(in this case) | The A register can be commanded to furnish data: in this case the central computer sends this command. |
| similar / in . . . fashion<br>(in) . . . (fashion) (Similarly,) | In similar fashion, an electron shot along path PDE takes spiral path PACS. |
| all / the diagram<br>(all) | The following symbols are used in all the diagrams in this report: . . . |
| their / appropriate<br>(appropriate) | The power-supply cabinet contains the beam power supply, the magnet power supply, and their appropriate line regulators. |
| highly / useful<br>(highly) | This technique is highly useful in detecting shorts. |
| enlarged / somewhat<br>(somewhat) | The computer system will be enlarged somewhat. |
| very / comprehensive<br>(very) | The control circuit includes a very comprehensive interlock system. |
| great / many<br>(a great) | We still have to study a great many other speech parameters. |

| | |
|---|---|
| it can operate / where necessary<br>(where necessary) ✓ | Because of its rugged construction, it can operate from rough, unprepared landing strips where necessary. |
| cost-engineering / nature<br>(a) ✓ . . (nature) ✓ | This report summarizes studies of a cost-engineering nature. |

COMMENT: IN DELETING "A" AND "NATURE" FROM THE SENTENCE IN THE PRECEDING FRAME, THE HYPHEN IN "COST-ENGINEERING" IS ALSO DELETED, SINCE IT IS NO LONGER A UNIT MODIFIER (SEE SECTION 14-4). THIS SENTENCE MIGHT BE BETTER WRITTEN:

. . . summarizes cost-engineering studies.

| | |
|---|---|
| Their / associated<br>(associated) ✓ | The synchronizer cabinet houses two synchronizers and their associated switching and monitoring circuits. |
| suitable / control words<br>(suitable) ✓ | The concentrator acts as directed by suitable control words. |
| space / available<br>(available) ✓ | The memory space available for sorting and for citation storage is 4,000 words. |
| active / developing<br>(active in) ✓ | The Viditronia Company has been active in developing video-processing techniques for many years. |

# FUNCTION WORDS, VERBS, AND LONG REDUNDANCIES

### 3-1   Function Words: "By," "As," "Of"

Function words such as "by," "as," and "of" give the relationships between words. When used unnecessarily, they are misleading. "Of" is not needed in:

We moved the crucible off (of) the stand.

"As" is superfluous in:

Carry out the trouble-shooting procedures in the order as listed below.

You will have little difficulty finding similar small and unnecessary words in the following sentences. When reviewing each frame, note the strong impact of these misleadingly small words.

*DELETE SUPERFLUOUS SMALL WORDS*

| | |
|---|---|
| successively / as<br>(as) | Each trunk group appears successively as green, yellow, and red. |
| off / of<br>(of) | We took the connectors off of the old convertors. |
| select / out<br>(out) | This circuit selects one out of the three drum heads. |

| | |
|---|---|
| passed / by<br>(by) | The needle had <u>passed</u> <u>by</u> the highest permissible value. |
| to serve / so as<br>(so as) | Components can be arranged so as to serve as crossovers. (Delete two words.) |
| passes / by<br>(by) | The envelope passes by the counter before the scanner. |
| use / as<br>(as) (or: the) | The airplane is available for the use as described above. |
| both / of the<br>(of the) | Both of the mock-ups have arrived. (Delete two words.) |

## 3-2 Verbs

Verbs are power words. They give sentences their "go." As a result, when they are superfluous, they emphatically misplace emphasis. For example, a statement that "water was boiled and heated" gives equal emphasis to the two activities, but only one of them need be mentioned, for boiling implies heating. In the following sentence underline the unnecessary verb:

**Station Alpha received and retransmitted the message from Station Gamma.**

The superfluous word is "received": retransmitting a message implies that the message has been received.

### DELETE SUPERFLUOUS VERBS

| | |
|---|---|
| has been progressing / is . . . complete<br>(has been progressing and) | The detailed logic design of the drum memory circuits has been progressing and is now 75 percent finished. |
| taken / decoded<br>(taken and) | The input PCM is <u>taken and decoded</u> into two PAM signals. |
| tabulate / present<br>(and present it) (To tabulate is to present in a table.) | The computer will <u>tabulate</u> the data <u>and present</u> it according to the frequency of events. |
| Press / hold down<br>(Press and) (or: and hold down) | Press and hold down the push button until the red light goes out. |
| contoured / fit<br>(are contoured to) (or: fit) | The viewing hoods are contoured to fit the face. |

COMMENT: REMOVING DEADWOOD OFTEN EXPOSES FAULTS THAT WOULD OTHERWISE REMAIN HIDDEN. IN THE FOLLOW-
ING SENTENCE, FOR EXAMPLE, IT APPEARS THAT BOTH "ABILITY" AND "CAPABILITY" ARE SUPERFLUOUS:

We checked the new model for reading ~~ability~~ and for paper handling ~~capability~~.

TO CHECK FOR READING IS TO CHECK FOR THE ABILITY TO READ. AND TO CHECK FOR PAPER HANDLING IS TO CHECK FOR
THE CAPABILITY OF HANDLING PAPER. BUT WHEN THESE WORDS ARE DELETED, IT BECOMES OBVIOUS THAT SOMETHING
IS MISSING. THE WRITER MUST HAVE MEANT SOMETHING ELSE, POSSIBLY SOMETHING LIKE:

We checked *how well* the new model read and *how well* it handled paper.

HAD THE WRITER REMOVED "ABILITY" AND CAPABILITY," HE WOULD HAVE SEEN HE WAS NOT GETTING ACROSS WHAT HE
INTENDED.

## 3-3  Other Verbs and Verb Derivatives

Verbs or words made from them repeat information in the following frames. In the
following sentence, "in the front panel" tells where the filters are "located":

Air passes through filters ~~located~~ in the front panel.

As you review the change, note how powerfully superfluous verb forms direct
attention.

### DELETE UNNECESSARY VERB FORMS

| | |
|---|---|
| presented / in <br> ~~presented~~ | The diagrams <u>presented</u> <u>in</u> this manual use the symbols below. |
| located / near <br> ~~located~~ | The transformer is <u>located</u> <u>near</u> the meter. |
| shown / on <br> ~~shown~~ | We set the amplitude of the points <u>shown</u> <u>on</u> the plot proportional to the time between zero crossings. |
| given / in <br> ~~given~~ | You need those tools for the tests given in this section. |
| stored / in <br> ~~stored~~ | This processor manipulates the data stored in the magnetic-core memory. |
| mounted / on <br> ~~mounted~~ | The circuit breakers are mounted on the front plates. |
| performing / switching <br> ~~performing (its)~~ | The card reader expends no power in performing its switching. |
| making / studies <br> ~~making~~ | The materials department has responsibility for making structural studies. |

| | |
|---|---|
| occurring / in<br>~~occurring~~ | This simulates a fault occurring in the Klystron circuits. |
| by / using<br>~~using~~ | The number of channels can be reduced by using time multiplexing. |
| used / for checking<br>~~used~~ | These are the jacks used for checking the panel meters. |

## 3-4 Longer Redundancies

Most of the superfluous expressions in the preceding frames were of one word. In the following, they are of at least two words—usually more:

| | |
|---|---|
| approaches / that can be taken<br>~~that can be taken~~ | This section discusses approaches that can be taken to retrieving citations. |
| steps / accomplished<br>~~that must be accomplished~~ | There are eight steps that must be accomplished in this conversion. |
| use of / a . . . semiconductor<br>~~the use of~~ | The use of a variable-gas semiconductor satisfies these requirements. |
| be such as to / must . . . provide<br>~~be such as to~~ | The design must be such as to give positive spring action. |
| use in / for . . . devices<br>~~use in~~ | We are now preparing thin films for use in active devices. |
| is one / consists<br>~~is one that~~ (or, ~~that consists~~) | The recommended structure is one that consists of alternate layers of semiconductor and metal. |
| amplifier / amplifier<br>~~is an amplifier that~~ | A power amplifier is an amplifier that delivers high power as opposed to high voltage or high current. |
| is in . . . form / it requires<br>~~is in such a form that it~~ | The modification kit is in such a form that it requires no tools. |
| The controller / is a unit<br>~~is a unit that~~ | The controller is a unit that enables the TDM operator to test all sets from one position. |
| use / a high temperature<br>~~the use of~~ | The use of a high temperature is necessary for thermodynamic equilibrium. |

The long superfluous expressions end the following sentences:

| | |
|---|---|
| enable / accomplished<br>(to be accomplished) | Command consoles on each communications loop enable alternate routing to be accomplished. |
| used singly / . . . is required<br>(to suit circumstance in which only)<br>(one is required.) | Each of the concentrators can be used singly to suit circumstances in which only one is required. (Very long.) |
| light-tight / no . . . light<br>(in which there were no detectable)<br>(light leaks.) | The result was a light-tight enclosure, in which there were no detectable light leaks. |
| prevents frost / when . . . is too low<br>(when the temperature is low)<br>(enough to form frost.) | The heater prevents frost when the temperature is low enough to form frost. (It could not do it any other time.) |
| can be repeated / if . . . desirable<br>(if future needs indicate that this is)<br>(desirable.) | These experiments can be repeated if future needs indicate that this is desirable. |

The deadwood in the following sentences are split by words that are not to be removed, as in:

This policy takes care of (occasions when) accidents (occur)

| | |
|---|---|
| failure / occurred<br>(that). . .(has occurred) | The red light indicates that a failure has occurred. |
| redundancy / remained<br>(that). . .(remained) | A preliminary study revealed that much redundancy remained. |
| handles / generated<br>(the situation where). . .(are gen-)<br>(erated) | The rounding-off routine handles the situation where fractions are generated. |
| is not . . . restricted / required<br>. . . approach<br>(required to take). .(an approach) | This computer is not required to take so restricted an approach. (Keep negative: "not.") |

## 3-5  Other Deadwood

In the following sentences are deadwood that do not fit with any of the preceding. Nevertheless, you will find them easily.

## DELETE DEADWOOD

| | |
|---|---|
| simplest / simple <br> (simple) | One of the simplest is the simple cantilever spring contact. |
| acoustical / noise <br> (acoustical) | The acoustical noise should be reduced. ("Acoustical" refers to sound.) |
| current / electricity <br> (electricity) | These lines connect to alternating current electricity. (Alternating current is a kind of electricity.) |
| surface / side <br> (the surface of ) | The vent is on the surface of the side. |
| link / together <br> (together) | Printed wires link together the test points. |
| hold / in store <br> (in store) | What does the future hold in store? |
| economical / cost <br> (in terms of cost) | The approved method is economical in terms of cost. |
| use / soap <br> (the use of) | The use of soap aids in cleaning. |
| means of / by changing <br> (means of ) | Channels are reassigned by means of changing the crystal and retuning. |
| two signals / separate <br> (separate) | The data is decoded into two separate signals. |
| aid / setup <br> (the aid of) | Sulfide deposition was controlled by the aid of the optical setup described earlier. |
| deposits / grease or oil <br> (deposits of) | Remove deposits of grease or oil with a solvent and a soft cloth. |
| means / vibrators <br> (means of ) | The powder is fed to the heater by <u>means</u> of <u>vibrators</u>. |
| at . . . sites / location <br> (location of ) | The civil engineers bored test holes at the location of building and antenna sites. |
| vibration and shock / forces <br> (forces) | This isolation attenuates vibration and shock forces. |
| knowledge / information <br> (information) (or, (knowledge of) ) | Knowledge of the format location is enough information. |

| | |
|---|---|
| dust / accumulation<br>(accumulation) | Remove dust accumulation. |
| aid of / with . . . ohmeter<br>(the aid of) | Check continuity with the aid of an ohmeter. |
| the art of / speech-bandwidth reduction<br>(the art of) | In the present state of the art of speech-bandwidth reduction, such error probabilities are objectionable. |
| Thus, / in summary<br>(Thus) (or: (in summary)) | Thus, in summary, we can reduce the weight. |
| a few / additional<br>(additional) (or: (A few additional)) | A few additional spare tracks should be added. |
| 140 milliamperes / current<br>(of current) | The "write" amplifier delivers 140 milliamperes of current to the drumhead. (A milliampere is a unit of current.) |
| panel / ten listeners<br>(a panel of) ("ten listeners" is more precise) | A panel of ten listeners took the preference test. |
| coating / material<br>(material) | The final coating material depends on the following: |
| adjustment / requirements<br>(requirements) (adjustments) | The central control eliminates manual adjustment requirements. (Rewrite slightly.) |
| logic circuits / various<br>(various) | The various logic circuits determine how the message concentrator responds to programmed instructions and control words. |
| equipment / equipment<br>(from an equipment standpoint) | This is important from an equipment standpoint because it limits the equipment needed. |

COMMENT: A MISLEADING MESSAGE WAS CARRIED BY AN UNNECESSARY WORD IN THE FOLLOWING SENTENCE:

Zero the meter needle *mechanically* with a small screwdriver.

"MECHANICALLY" SUGGESTED THERE WAS IMPORTANCE TO A DISTINCTION BETWEEN THIS SCREWDRIVER ADJUSTMENT AND OTHER ADJUSTMENTS, THUS DEVELOPING IN THE READER AN EXPECTATION OF LEARNING ABOUT IT. YET THERE WAS NO OTHER ADJUSTMENT; "MECHANICAL" WAS WHOLLY SUPERFLUOUS. AS A RESULT, THE READER'S EXPECTATION WAS NEVER SATISFIED. HE WAS LEFT WITH A VAGUE, UNSATISFIED ANTICIPATION.

## 3-6 Review

Continue reviewing each frame.

## DELETE DEADWOOD

| | |
|---|---|
| listed / in the request<br>(listed) | This brake satisfies the specifications listed in the Request for Proposal. |
| means of / heater<br>(means of) | The temperature is kept constant by means of a tantalum-strip heater. |
| off / of<br>(of) | These figures were taken off of the dial. |
| located / at the rear<br>(located) | The output ends on bus bars located at the rear of the cabinet. |
| exist that / are<br>(exist that) | Some practicable formulas exist that are easier to handle. |
| appearing / in<br>(appearing) | You can connect the test equipment through the test jacks to any circuit appearing in the audio bay. |
| as / specified<br>(as) | Our filter satisfies the environmental conditions as specified in their standards. |
| acoustical / noise<br>(acoustical) | To reduce acoustical noise, we coated the inner surface with a sound-deadening material. |
| human / utterances<br>(human) | We will then gather the parameters from human utterances of words. |
| for / use in<br>(use in) | The pilot-tone transmitter generates a 10-kilohertz tone for use in the system. |
| greasy or oily / material<br>(material) (Remove grease or oil) | Remove greasy or oily material with a solvent. (Rewrite slightly.) |
| all / of<br>(of) (or: All of) | The monitor samples all of the signals during each cycle. |
| aid / ammeter<br>(the aid of) | Measure the current with the aid of an ammeter. |
| means / connections<br>(means of) | Trouble indicators on the supervisory console are activated by means of lines from the maintenance console. |
| human / face<br>(human) | The radar-screen viewing hood fits the human face. |
| for a twin check / to be accomplished<br>(to be accomplished) | For a twin check to be accomplished, overlap the data one clock pulse. |

| | |
|---|---|
| use / opening <br> (the use of) | Feed the coolant into the heat exchanger through the use of the opening in the top. |
| aid / connection <br> (the aid of) | Check continuity with the aid of the wire-connection list and the cabling diagram. |
| punching / of <br> (of)(the first "of") | Avoid punching of mounting holes within 0.1 inch of each other. |
| cost standpoint / in price <br> (From the cost standpoint) (or: (in) price) | From the cost standpoint there is no appreciable difference in price. |
| the results / obtained <br> (obtained) | This reports the results obtained so far. |
| use / evaporation <br> (The use of) | The use of "flash" evaporation offers a different way of studying such complex materials. |
| using / contacts <br> (Using)(Ring contacts *do* not lower) | Using ring contacts does not lower series resistance as much as originally thought. ("Does" becomes "do.") |
| the one / performed <br> (has been performed) | No further tests need be made after the one in paragraph 64 has been performed. |
| use / transformer <br> (the use of) | The measurement was made without the use of a transformer. |
| to indicate / that addresses should be sent <br> (to indicate) | The recorder then sends a signal to indicate that addresses should be sent. |
| can be modified / if . . . requirements change <br> (if performance requirements) (change) | The assembly language can be modified easily if performance requirements change. |

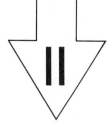

# UNLEASHING
# VERB POWER

Verbs are sentence muscle—action words. For vigorous prose they have to be free—giving direct, immediate impact. The following chapters will help you achieve this immediacy. They show how to write actively and with dynamic verbs. The result will be action writing.

# PREFERRING ACTIVE VOICE

The passive voice is indispensible for a flexible style. But active voice is more direct and forceful and is usually to be preferred.

Active voice is so named because the emphasis is on someone or something acting. In passive voice the emphasis is on someone or something being passively acted upon. The following sentence is in the active voice, because the subject, (single underline) "he," acts:

He turned the key.

The verb (double underline) says something about the subject. It tells what "he" did. Since "he" acted, the verb is active in voice.

The following sentence is passive: its subject, "the key," is acted upon:

The key was turned.

The key does nothing, but somehow it gets turned. The actor, the one who does the turning, is not even mentioned. The following sentence is passive also:

The key was turned by him.

Here, though the actor is mentioned, the subject, "the key," still is passive.

Keep in mind that the advice here is to prefer active voice, not to use it exclusively. As observed earlier, passive voice is indispensible. Use it to deemphasize the actor ("him," "he"), or to direct attention to the act ("was turned"), or to stress the subject receiving the action ("the key"). Otherwise, favor the active voice; wherever the context permits, have somebody or something do something. The following frames will help you distinguish between active and passive voice. Cover the left half now. Circle "Active" or "Passive." Then check left.

## CIRCLE "ACTIVE" OR "PASSIVE" AS THE SUBJECT ACTS OR IS PASSIVE

| Passive | Subject    Verb |
| | Control is centered in the operations-control area. |
| | Active          Passive |

| Passive | The threshold level was lowered corre-spondingly. |
| | Active          Passive |

| Active | Four parallel branch currents flow through V-1. |
| | Active          Passive |

| Passive | They are housed in the larger building. |
| | Active          Passive |

COMMENT: NOTE IN THE PRECEDING FRAMES THAT PASSIVE-VOICE VERBS HAVE A TWO-PART FORM: (1) A "BE" VERB, SUCH AS "IS," "ARE," "WAS," AND "WERE"; AND (2) ANOTHER VERB THAT ENDS IN "-ED": "IS CENTERED," "WAS LOWERED," AND "ARE HOUSED." OTHER EXAMPLES ARE "WILL BE CALLED" AND "HAD BEEN HANDLED."

ALL PASSIVE-VOICE VERBS HAVE THIS TWO-PART PATTERN. BUT SOME DO NOT END IN "-ED," FOR EXAMPLE, "ARE SHOWN," "WERE GIVEN," "WILL BE KEPT," AND "WAS MADE." EVEN THOUGH SOME DO NOT END IN "-ED," YOU CAN ALWAYS DETERMINE VOICE BY OBSERVING WHETHER THE SUBJECT ACTS OR IS PASSIVE.

## CONTINUE CIRCLING "ACTIVE" OR "PASSIVE" AS THE SUBJECT ACTS OR IS PASSIVE

| Passive (*is* connected) | The common point is connected to ground through the speed-regulator circuits. |
| | Active          Passive |

| Passive (a non-"ed" passive) | A thorough consideration has been given to their views. |
| | Active          Passive |

| Active | The first section did control the logic unit. |
| | Active          Passive |

| Passive (must *be* rejected) | As much signal interference as possible must be rejected by the receiver. |
| | Active          Passive |

| | |
|---|---|
| Passive<br>(can *be* converted) | The current <u>can be converted</u> by the first diode. |

| | Active | Passive |
|---|---|---|
| 1. Active (past tense)<br>2. Active | (1) <u>We hoped</u> that (2) <u>we could determine</u> the degree of mixing. | |
| | (1) Active | Passive |
| | (2) Active | Passive |

COMMENT: NOTE THAT PASSIVE VOICE HAS NOTHING TO DO WITH PAST TIME. VOICE DEALS ONLY WITH WHETHER THE SUBJECT ACTS OR IS ACTED UPON WITHOUT REGARD TO WHEN. IN THE PRECEDING FRAME, "WE HOPED THAT. . . ." REFERS TO AN ACTIVITY THAT TOOK PLACE AT A PAST TIME; YET "HOPED" IS ACTIVE IN VOICE BECAUSE AT THAT PAST TIME THE SUBJECT, "WE," ACTED: "WE" DID THE HOPING.

## 4-1   Simple Changes from Passive Voice

Rewrite verbs in the following problem sentences so that they are no longer passive. Place your hand over the left half now. Keep the same subject (single underline). Just rewrite the verb so that the subject acts:

"First, <u>the frame</u> <u>is dropped</u> . . ."

When reviewing the frames, note how the activity of the subject changes.

_REWRITE IN ACTIVE VOICE_

| | |
|---|---|
| The variable-speed motor<br>     connects<br>  (is connected) to the | The variable-speed motor <u>is connected</u> to the drive-transmission system through the magnetic clutch. |
| centers<br>Full control (is centered) in the . . . | Full control <u>is centered</u> in the operations-control area. |
| The impedance to ground<br>  increases<br>(is increased.) | The impedance to ground <u>is increased</u>. |
| combines<br>The error signal (is combined)<br>with . . . | The error signal <u>is combined</u> with the feedback signal. |
| feeds<br>The delayed trigger (is fed) into<br>a . . . | The delayed trigger <u>is fed</u> into a multivibrator. |

| | |
|---|---|
| The common point . . . ~~connects~~ ~~(is connected)~~ to ground . . . | The common point of the saturable reactor and the detector is connected to ground through speed-regulator circuits. |
| The "Return on Investment" col- ~~applies~~ umn ~~(is applied)~~ in | The "Return on Investment" column is applied in only one case. |
| lowers The threshold level ~~(is lowered)~~ correspondingly. | The threshold level is lowered correspondingly. |
| connect Major signals . . . ~~(are connected)~~ to | Major signals, such as receiver and transmitter bit rates, are connected to these test points. |

## 4-2  Transposing Old and New Subjects

To become active in voice, some sentences need new subjects. Create the active voice by transposing the original and the new subject:

The crop values are summarized in Table 1.

Table 1 summarizes the crop values.

The old and the new subject interchange positions on either side of the verb, which itself merely changes in voice. Rewrite the following sentences similarly. Upper left gives the new subject, should you run into difficulties. Lower left gives the correct revision.

## REWRITE IN ACTIVE VOICE

| | |
|---|---|
| Appendix D Appendix D describes the station. | The station is described in Appendix D. Appendix D |
| The new components The new components simplify the extraction. | The extraction is simplified by the new components. The new components |
| The ammeter The ammeter measures the current. | The current is measured by the ammeter. The ammeter |

COMMENT: IN MANY OF THE REMAINING FRAMES, THERE ARE NO UNDERLINES. TO GUIDE YOURSELF IN WORKING WITH THEM, FIRST FIND THE VERB: IT SAYS SOMETHING ABOUT SOMETHING. DOUBLE-UNDERLINE IT. THEN FIND THE SUBJECT BY ASKING, "WHO OR WHAT DOES WHAT THE VERB ASSERTS?" IN THE PRECEDING FRAME, "WHAT (OR WHO) IS MEASURED?" THE CURRENT IS. IN THE FRAME BEFORE THAT, "WHAT (WHO) IS SIMPLIFIED?" THE EXTRACTION IS.

---

A twin-tee filter

A twin-tee filter follows the amplifier.

The amplifier is followed by a twin-tee filter.

---

Flash evaporation

Flash evaporation offers a different approach. . . .

A different approach to studying these materials is offered by flash evaporation.

---

This circuit

This circuit includes a variable-gain control.

A variable-gain control is included in this circuit.

---

The design

The design establishes the reliability of a system.

The reliability of a system is established by the design.

---

The phase detector

The phase detector compares the I-F signals. . . .

The I-F signals from the two receivers are compared by the phase detector.

---

The exploratory work

The exploratory work will use the same method.

The same method will be used in the exploratory work. (Keep future time; use "will.")

---

A single antenna with . . .

A single antenna with . . . accomplishes this type of . . .

This type of transmission is accomplished by a single antenna with dual-feed horns.

---

The need to . . .

The need to reduce mismatch will govern the selection of . . .

The selection of an isostructural substrate will be governed by the need to reduce mismatch.

---

Figure 3

Figure 3 shows the three photographs.

The three photographs are shown in Figure 3.

---

Section 4

Section 4 describes the experience of our company

The experience of our company in similar studies is described in Section 4.

---

## 4-3  New Subject from an Introductory Phrase

The new subjects for the following sentences are in phrases that begin with prepositions like "in," "by," and "for" (prepositional phrases). These phrases are usually at the beginning of the sentence, as is the one italicized in the following sentence:

*In each picture* **the responses** **are shown.**

Removing the preposition brings out the new subject: "(In)each picture the. . . .": "Each picture" is the new subject:

**Each picture** shows **the responses.**

In the following sentences, work only on the italicized material.

## DELETE THE PREPOSITION, AND UNDERLINE THE NEW SUBJECT

| | |
|---|---|
| (For) Systems such as GaSb:InAs . . . | (For) *systems such as GaSb:InAs,* finer resolution is called for. |
| (In) the following discussion . . . | *In the following discussion* the theory of operation is given. |
| However, (for) the final test . . . | However, *for the final test* four cycles were analyzed. |
| (For) Alternate II . . . | *For Alternate II* no increase in scanning rate is needed. |
| (By) this . . . | *By this* the project manager is kept informed. |

Some of the following sentences are those you have just worked on. Rewrite them now in the active voice, taking new subjects from prepositional phrases. Should you run into difficulties, the new subjects are given at the upper left. When reviewing each frame note not only the change in emphasis but also how the change to active voice continues the shortening of sentences begun in the preceding unit. It drops the "be" verb and replaces the "-ed" verb with a shorter one. In the following sentences active voice also drops the preposition before the new subject.

## REWRITE IN ACTIVE VOICE

| | |
|---|---|
| the following discussion<br>The following discussion gives the theory of. . . . | (In) the following *discussion* the theory of operation is given. |
| our Rocky Mountain plant<br>Our Rocky Mountain plant manufactures special . . . | (At) *our Rocky Mountain plant* special electronic test and operational equipment is manufactured. |

| | |
|---|---|
| the final test<br>However, <u>the final test</u> <u>used</u> four | However, *for the final test* four cycles were used.<br><br>However, |
| Alternate II<br>Alternate II <u>requires</u> no increase in . . . | *For Alternate II* no increase in the scanning rate is required.<br><br>(Keep the tense present.) |
| our plans<br>Our plans <u>have</u> <u>given</u> attention to using the . . . | *In our plans* attention has been given to using the present catwalks.<br><br>(Use a form of "has" with the new verb.) |
| the original design<br>The original design <u>did not call</u> for monitor jacks. | *In the original design* monitor jacks were not called for.<br><br>(Keep the negative.) |
| an adequate bias<br>Thus, <u>an adequate bias</u> <u>can make</u> this current negligible. | Thus, *by an adequate bias* this current can be made negligible. Thus,<br><br>(Use "can" with the verb.) |
| systems such as GaSb:InAs<br>Systems such as GaSb:InAs <u>needed</u> finer resolution. | *For systems such as GaSb:InAs,* finer resolution was needed.<br><br>(Keep the past tense.) |

## 4-4 Sentences Having Both Active and Passive Verbs

The following sentences have both an active-voice verb (A.V.) and a passive-voice verb (P.V.). Rewrite only the passive-voice verb, changing it to active.

*REWRITE IN ACTIVE VOICE*

| | |
|---|---|
| two factors<br>. . . show that <u>two factors</u> <u>cause</u> the difference in resistance. | (A.V.)<br>Electron microscope photographs show that<br>(P.V.)<br>the difference in resistance <u>is caused</u> by two factors.<br><br>. . . show that <u>two factors</u> _____ the difference . . . |

| | |
|---|---|
| the receiver | (A.V.) |
| . . . that <u>the receiver</u> <u>rejects</u> as much interference as possible. | The time constant must be large enough that <br> (P.V.) <br> as much interference as possible <u>is rejected</u> by the receiver. <br><br> . . . that <u>the receiver</u> |
| the diode | (A.V.) |
| . . . that <u>the diode</u> <u>can deliver</u>. | We are calculating the photo-current that <br> (P.V.) <br> can be delivered by the diode. <br><br> . . . that <u>the diode</u> can |
| back-biased diodes | (A.V.) |
| . . . that <u>back-biased diodes</u> <u>impose</u> on power. | Several authors have discussed the limitations <br> (P.V.) <br> that are imposed on power by back-biased diodes. <br><br> . . . that back-biased diodes |
| that the new vocoder reduces <br> <u>That the new vocoder reduces</u> <br> . . . <u>substantiates</u> this conclusion. | (P.V.) <br> This conclusion is substantiated in that the <br> (A.V.) <br> new vocoder reduces differences. <br><br> That the new vocoder reduces . . . |
| that the sample <br> . . . that <u>the sample</u> <u>shall not</u> deviate from the basic design. | The purchase description specifies that the <br> (P.V.) <br> basic design shall not be deviated from in the sample. <br><br> . . . that |
| the highest voltage . . . flows <br> <u>The highest voltage</u> . . . <u>does not limit</u> the depth . . . | The depth of modulation is not limited by the highest voltage possible before current flows. <br><br> The highest voltage . . . does not |
| <u>the two stations</u> (that) <br> . . . for <u>the two stations that</u> <u>use</u> 1-kilowatt-hour amplifiers. | We supplied vans for the two stations where 1-kilowatt-power amplifiers <u>are used</u>. <br><br> . . . for the two stations that |

## 4-5 Review

In the following frames are all the preceding types of passive-voice sentences. Change them to active. Upper left gives the subject, should you need that clue.

Up to this point, upper left has usually given the complete subject. From now on, it will usually give only the simple subject, the simple subject being the most important word in the complete subject. In the preceding frame, the complete subject is "the two stations." The simple subject is "stations." Continue reviewing each frame.

## REWRITE IN ACTIVE VOICE

---

circuit
The circuit includes a protective. . . .

A protective series resistance is included in the circuit.

---

The material
The material . . . passes into the heater . . .

The material to be evaporated is passed into the heater as fine grains.

The material  to be evaporated

---

clutch / motor
Normally, the clutch engages . . . the motor energizes.

Normally, the clutch is engaged at the same time the motor is energized.

---

. . . (the van) which . . .
. . . in the van which houses the other equipment.

They are in the van in which the other equipment is housed.

. . . the van which

---

indexing
Indexing uses only . . .

Only 28 locator words are used for indexing.

---

clock pulses
Clock pulses gate the . . . signal.

The quantized signal is gated by clock pulses.

---

decreasing
Decreasing the maximum value provides some benefits.

Some benefits are provided by decreasing the maximum value.

Decreasing the . . .

---

(a reader) which
. . . into a reader which connects to a typing perforator.

The intercept operator inserts the tape from the perforator into a reader which is connected to a typing perforator.

. . . into a reader which

---

the signal
The signal needs those extra . . .

Those extra bits are needed by the signal for fidelity.

---

ordinance
This ordinance imposes a tax on. . . .

Under this ordinance is imposed a tax on cigarettes, cigars, and tobacco.

This ordinance

---

Table IV
Table IV lists the lattice parameters. . . .

The lattice parameters for different compositions are listed in Table IV.

Table IV

| | |
|---|---|
| **reliance** | The probability of detecting targets <u>is decreased</u> because of the heavy reliance on the operator. |
| The heavy reliance . . . <u>decreases</u> the probability of . . . (or: The probability . . . <u>decreases</u> because of . . .) | |
| | The heavy reliance on the operator |
| **signal** | The signal <u>is fed</u> into a multivibrator which generates a 5,000-meter gate. |
| The signal <u>feeds</u> into a multivibrator which. . . . | |
| | The signal |
| **appendix** | The triangulation is described in an appendix to this report. |
| An appendix to this report <u>describes</u> the triangulation. | |
| | An appendix to . . . |
| . . . (show that) this device | Our studies show that with this device the coupling loss can be significantly reduced. |
| . . . show that <u>this device</u> <u>can</u> significantly <u>reduce</u> the coupling loss. | |
| | . . . show that <u>this device</u> can significantly |
| . . . (so that) all | Align the tubes so that all <u>are heated</u> at the same time. |
| . . . so that <u>all</u> <u>heat</u> at the same time. | |
| **Flash evaporation** | With flash evaporation, depositable semiconductors <u>are increased</u> to include the III-IV compounds. |
| Flash evaporation <u>increases</u> depositable semiconductors. . . . | |
| | Flash evaporation |
| **TIVAL** | These cards <u>are used</u> by TIVAL to convert the digitally coded speech to sound. |
| <u>TIVAL</u> <u>uses</u> these cards to . . . | |
| | TIVAL |
| **section** | All tools, test equipment, special cables, jigs, and fixtures are listed in this section. |
| This <u>section</u> <u>lists</u> all tools. . . . | |
| **stations** | The basic system is augmented by secondary stations. |
| Secondary stations <u>augment</u> the basic system. | |

COMMENT: SOME COMMENTATORS RECOMMEND THE USE OF PASSIVE VOICE IN ENGINEERING AND TECHNICAL WRITING ON THE GROUND THAT ITS IMPERSONALITY MATCHES THE IMPERSONAL CHARACTER OF TECHNOLOGY. BUT SCIENTIFIC AND ENGINEERING WRITING HAVE AS THEIR PRIMARY AIM THE DIRECT, IMMEDIATE COMMUNICATION OF INFORMATION. EINSTEIN, NEWTON, DARWIN, AND OTHER GREAT SCIENTISTS DESCRIBED THEIR WORK ACTIVELY WHEN IT BEST CONVEYED THEIR INFORMATION. NO ONE WRITING ON TECHNICAL SUBJECTS SHOULD FEAR TO FOLLOW THEIR EXAMPLE.

| | |
|---|---|
| **position** | The oscillator frequency is modulated by the position of the gyro. |
| The position of the gyro modulates the . . . | |

| | |
|---|---|
| manual | The equipment at these sites is described in this manual. |
| This manual describes the equipment. . . . | |
| bias | By a high enough bias, this current can be decreased. |
| A high enough bias can decrease this current. | |
| station | Its master tone will not be received at the second station. |
| The second station will not receive its. . . . | |
| arrangements | More read heads are needed on parallel arrangements. |
| Parallel arrangements need more read heads. | |
| display | The target size is optimized by the square display. |
| The square display optimizes the target. . . . | |

# REPLACING WEAK VERBS: "BE," "DO," "MAKE"

Lively verbs that picture activities often hide behind imprecise verbs such as "be," "do," and "make." The following chapters will help you bring out these dynamic descriptive verbs.

### 5-1 "Be" Verb: New Verb following the "Be" Verb

The following sentence relies on the verb "is":

"Is" acts as little more than an "equals" sign, merely linking the expressions on either side of it. Yet, "is a list of" conceals a highly descriptive verb: "lists" can replace "is":

Table 4 ~~is a list of~~ **lists** the accept and error rates.

This carries the same message, but more dramatically.

The verbs in the following frames are also forms of "be," such as "is," "are," "was," "were," "will be," and "have been." As in the example sentence above, the potential verb follows the "be" verb; thus, "is a list of" became "lists," and "is in excess of" becomes "exceeds." Try to replace "are" in the following sentence with a new verb made from a word that follows it.

These sections ~~are an explanation of~~ how to adjust the output.

The potential verb is "explanation." You should have changed it to "explain."

These sections **explain** how to adjust the output.

Revise the following sentences similarly, being sure to remove all unnecessary words before checking left. Note that potential verbs are in italics.

## REPLACE FORMS OF "BE" WITH DESCRIPTIVE VERBS

| | |
|---|---|
| Table 2 lists the. . . . | Table 2 is a list of the launchers delivered. |
| These reports explain the. . . . | These reports are an explanation of the tests. |

**COMMENT: IN REVIEWING EACH FRAME, GIVE SPECIAL ATTENTION TO THE INCREASED DIRECTNESS OF THE NEW VERB.**

| | |
|---|---|
| These quantities exceed the. . . . | These quantities are in excess of the limits. |
| Present . . . transmission wastes bandwidth. | Present-day color television transmission is wasteful of bandwidth. |
| The pressure on . . . will depend on the. . . . | The pressure on the contacts will be dependent on the thickness. |
| Figure 3 illustrates the method of | Figure 3 is an illustration of the method of field assembly of the bridge. |
| He supervised the . . . | He was supervisor of the drilling at site A. |

Single underlines in the following sentences indicate subjects. In some sentences the old and new verbs are in italics. Before checking left, carefully read the revised sentence to be sure you have removed all unnecessary words.

| | |
|---|---|
| This reverses the. . . . | This is the reverse of the standard placement. |
| The following text briefly describes a. . . . | The following text is a brief description of a saturable reactor. |
| | (Use "briefly.") |
| The rise time . . . coincides with the turn-on time. | The rise time of the point-target echo is coincident with the turn-on time. |
| Mr. Jones manages the. . . . | Mr. Jones is the manager of the engineering section. |
| These records will aid greatly in documenting the system. | These records will be a great aid in documenting the system. |
| | These records will _____ greatly in. . . . |

| | |
|---|---|
| The . . . processor controls communications. | The input-output processor is a control on communications. |

## 5-2 "Be" Verb: New Verb in the Original Subject

In the following sentences you have to make new verbs from their original subject:

<u>Examination</u> of the reason for this decline must be made.

The reason for this decline must be examined.

(1) The new subject comes from an "of" phrase that follows the main part of the original subject: "of the reason for this decline." (The "of" phrase and the main part of the original subject make up the complete subject.) (2) The new verb comes from the main part of the original subject: "Examination" — often called the simple subject. Revise the following sentence before reading on:

<u>Operation</u> of the calibrator is as follows:

Do not read on until you finish your revision. You should have written:

The calibrator operates as follows:

Now review these changes so you can make similar changes in the following frames. The clues in the upper left frames are the new subjects with the potential verb in parentheses. For the preceding example sentences, upper left would be: Calibrator (operation). This gives us "The calibrator operates. . . ." Single underlines indicate the new subject—which may or may not be the original subject. Italics identify original and potential verbs.

### REWRITE WITH DYNAMIC VERBS

| | |
|---|---|
| These authors (contention) <br> These authors contend that . . . | The contention of these authors is that the following will happen. <br> These authors |
| This team (conclusion) <br> This team concluded that . . . | The conclusion of this team was that our manuals are not clearly written. |
| The guide (alignment) <br> The guide was aligned accurately. | The alignment of the guide was accurate. (Use "accurately.") |
| The report will be (Divisions) <br> The report will be divided by topics. | Divisions of the report will be by topics. |

| | |
|---|---|
| This formula (use) | The use of this formula is in solving elastic-foundation problems. |
| This formula <u>is used</u> in solving. . . . | |

## 5-3 "Be" Verb: A Mix of the Preceding Types of "Be" Verb

The following frames have sentences of the two preceding types. Underlines continue to point up new subjects.

### REPLACE FORMS OF "BE" WITH DYNAMIC VERBS

| | |
|---|---|
| <u>criteria</u> (agreement) | These criteria are in agreement with those for telephone systems. |
| These <u>criteria</u> <u>agree</u> with those for. . . . | |
| The power source (connection) | Connection of <u>the power source</u> was through power-distribution panels in each van. |
| <u>The power source</u> (was) <u>connected</u> through . . . | |
| <u>It</u> (serviceable) | <u>It</u> is serviceable in keeping the series resistance low. |
| <u>It</u> <u>serves</u> in keeping the . . . | |
| <u>This approach</u> (result) from | <u>This approach</u> *is the result of* our study of the human perceptual process. (Use "from.") |
| <u>This approach</u> <u>resulted</u> (results) from our. . . . | |
| Phase-lock loops (use) | The first use of <u>phase-lock loops</u> was in synchronizing television receivers. |
| <u>Phase-lock loops</u> <u>were</u> first <u>used</u> in. . . . | |
| <u>The choice</u> of the final coating (dependent) | <u>The choice of the final coating</u> is dependent on the following: |
| <u>The choice of</u> . . . <u>depends</u> on the. . . . | |

The following sentences need slightly more rewriting. Cross out the original verb. Then make sense of what remains. Do your best to rewrite the sentences before checking left.

### REWRITE WITH NEW VERBS

| | |
|---|---|
| <u>The problem</u> of . . . will (continuing) | <u>The problem of obtaining transportation</u> will be a continuing one. |
| <u>The problem</u> of . . . <u>will continue</u>. | |

| | |
|---|---|
| An amplifier (following) _____<br>An amplifier <u>follows</u> the low-pass filter. | Following the low-pass filter is <u>an amplifier</u>. |
| They (participation) _____<br>They will (have to) <u>participate</u> as | Their participation will be as needed.<br>They <u>will</u> |
| The speed (triple) _____<br>The speed will about <u>triple</u>. | The increase in speed will be about triple.<br>The <u>speed</u> will about |
| These soils (study) _____<br>These soils are being <u>studied</u>. | These soils are under study.<br>These soils _____ being |

COMMENT: IN THE SENTENCE YOU HAVE JUST WRITTEN, "ARE" IS AN AUXILIARY VERB (A HELPING VERB). IT WORKS IN CONJUNCTION WITH THE MAIN VERB, "STUDIED." IN THE ORIGINAL SENTENCE "ARE" WAS THE MAIN SENTENCE VERB.

| | |
|---|---|
| These alloys (different) _____<br>These alloys <u>differ</u> in their resistance. . . . | These alloys *are different* in their resistance to corrosion. |
| transmission (change) _____<br><u>Transmission</u> <u>changes</u> linearly with . . . | Change of <u>transmission</u> with voltage is linear. (Use "linearly.") |
| All circuit breakers (trip) _____<br>All <u>circuit breakers</u> <u>trip</u> magnetically. | All circuit breakers are of the magnetic-trip type.<br>All circuit breakers _____ magnetically. |

## 5-4 "Make"

"Make" is another weak verb that often deadens sentence power, as in:

<u>This type of construction</u> <u>makes</u> *provision* (**provides**) **for future additions.**

The following sentences are like the example sentence: They keep the original subject. The potential verb follows the "make" verb: "makes provision" becomes "provides." Upper left gives the subject and potential verb. Check to be sure you are on the right track.

### REPLACE "MAKE" VERBS WITH MORE DYNAMIC ONES

| | |
|---|---|
| The receiver at . . . stations (connections) _____<br>The receiver at . . . <u>connects</u> with. . . . | The <u>receiver</u> at the central communication stations *makes connections* with the trunk lines. |

| | |
|---|---|
| As a . . . <u>you</u> (checkouts) <br><br> As a . . . <u>you</u> will be checking out (will check out) microwave systems. | As a systems technician <u>you</u> *will be making checkouts* on microwave systems. |
| Collection efficiency (increase) <br><br> Collection efficiency can be increased by. . . . | Collection efficiency *can be made to increase* by using a thermionic emitter. |
| The leads on the wafer (contact) <br> The leads on the wafer do not contact the pins . . . | The <u>leads</u> on the wafer *do not make contact* with the pins on the third layer. |
| [You] (corrections) <br> Correct the proof sheets with . . . | *Make corrections* on the proof sheets with standard proofreader's marks. <br> (The subject is "you," understood: "[You] Make corrections. . . .") |
| This characteristic . . . (simple) <br><br> This characteristic . . . simplifies parameter extraction. | This <u>characteristic</u> of the extractor *makes* parameter extraction *simple*. |
| . . . astronauts (changes) <br><br> . . . astronauts can change course in space. | With this device <u>astronauts</u> *can make* course *changes* in space. |

The new subjects for the following sentences are usually in "of" phrases that follow the original simple subject. The new verbs come from the original subjects.

| | |
|---|---|
| The present setup will (modifications) <br> The present setup will be modified. | Modifications of the present setup will be made. <br> The present setup will be |
| these displays (evaluation) <br> These displays will be evaluated during the. . . . | An evaluation of these displays will be made during the design phase. <br> These displays will be |
| subcontractors (selection) <br> Subcontractors will be selected in. . . . | Selection of subcontractors will be made in January. |
| Blackbody NEP (measurement) <br> Blackbody NEP was measured at. . . . | A measurement of blackbody NEP was made at zero bias and at a back bias of 0.5 milliampere. <br><br> (Keep the tense past.) |

COMMENT: THE POTENTIAL VERBS IN THE LAST FOUR FRAMES ENDED IN EITHER "-ION" OR "-ENT": "MODIFICAT*IONS*," "EVAL-UAT*ION*," "SELECT*ION*," AND "MEASUREM*ENT*." THESE ENDINGS OFTEN SIGNAL WEAKENED VERBS.

| | |
|---|---|
| This station (connec*tions*) ("-ion" ending) <br> This station will be connected with (will connect to) the other . . . | *Connections will be made* at <u>this station</u> with the other communications systems. |
| The crystal structure (examina-*tion*) ("-ion" ending) <br> The . . . structure was examined by. . . . | *Examination* of <u>the crystal structure</u> *was made* by x-ray microscopy. |

The following problem sentences may have either of the preceding patterns of revision. Continue reviewing each frame.

| | |
|---|---|
| The other coupling (Repairs) <br> The other coupling can be re-paired. | Repairs can be made to <u>the other coupling</u>. |
| The tape search (oscillate) <br> The tape search oscillates the tape reels. | <u>The tape search</u> makes the tape reels oscillate. |
| A system (recommenda*tion*) ("-ion" ending) <br> A system was recommended dur-ing. . . . | <u>A system</u> recommendation was made during phase 5. |
| Reliability (estimate) <br> Reliability will be estimated early. . . . | The estimate of reliability will be made early in the program. <br> Reliability will |
| No amount of (develop <br> No amount of feedback can de-velop a poor recognition system into . . . | <u>No amount of feedback</u> *can make* a poor recognition system *develop* into a good one. |
| This effect (measurem*ents*) ("-ent" ending) <br> This effect was not measured as a. . . . | No measurements were made of this effect as a function of R-F power. <br> <u>This effect</u> was not |
| . . . when these deflectors (ship-ment) <br> . . . when these deflectors are shipped. (or: . . . when you ship) | Notify the contracting officer when shipment is made of these deflectors. <br> Notify . . . when these deflectors |

| | |
|---|---|
| the two (match) | A better match can be made between <u>the two</u>. |
| The two <u>can be matched</u> better. | |

COMMENT: THE "-ION," "-ENT," AND SIMILAR WORDS ARE ABSTRACT NOUNS THAT NAME ACTIVITIES. THE NAMING TURNS THE ACTIVITY INTO AN INERT ABSTRACTION, AN ENTITY DEVOID OF MOVEMENT AND CHANGE. CONSIDER "MEASUREMENT" IN:

He made a measurement of the compression.

THE CONCEPT "MEASUREMENT" COVERS COUNTLESS ACTIVITIES FROM THE SCHOOL CHILD WITH HIS FOOT RULE TO THE TAILOR WITH HIS TAPE AND TO THE ASTRONOMER WITH HIS LIGHT YEARS. THE INDEFINITE VERB "MADE" BRINGS THE READER TO THIS BROAD SET OF MEANINGS AND JUST ABOUT ABANDONS HIM THERE. BUT WITH THE DYNAMIC VERB "MEASURED" THERE IS LIFE:

He measured the compression.

THIS VERB PICTURES A SPECIFIC ACTION, AND IT CARRIES THOUGHT FROM THE ACTOR DIRECTLY TO THE OBJECT OF HIS ACTION, BYPASSING THE HOST OF MEANINGS IN "MADE" AND IN "MEASUREMENT."

## 5-5 "Do"

Forms of the verb "do" stifle many potentially dynamic verbs, as in:

**He** *did design of* **(designed) the cofferdam.**

Develop other dynamic verbs in the following sentences in place of forms of "do," such as "did," "done," and "does." Check upper left for the subject and potential verb only if you run into difficulty or to check your rewriting before checking lower left.

### *REPLACE FORMS OF "DO" WITH DYNAMIC VERBS*

| | |
|---|---|
| Our staff (examinations) | <u>Our staff</u> *has done examinations on* this alloy. |
| Our staff <u>has examined</u> this alloy. | |
| The lead writer (review) | <u>The lead writer</u> does the review for technical accuracy and logical presentation. |
| The lead writer <u>reviews</u> for technical accuracy. . . . | |
| This machine (registering) | This machine does the registering of totals automatically. |
| This machine <u>registers</u> totals. . . . | |

COMMENT: THE NEW VERB IN THE PRECEDING FRAME CAME FROM THE PHRASE "THE REGISTERING OF." THIS PATTERN "THE . . . OF," "A . . . OF," AND OTHERS, SUCH AS "IN . . . OF," FREQUENTLY CONCEALS POTENTIAL VERBS, OFTEN IN "-ION" AND "-ENT" FORMS: *AN EXPLANATION OF* AND *THE MEASUREMENT OF.* BUT WE HAVE SEEN SOME POTENTIAL VERBS IN THESE PATTERNS THAT DID NOT HAVE "-ION" OR "-ENT" ENDINGS: "A STUDY OF" WAS ONE; "IN EXCESS OF" WAS ANOTHER.

| | |
|---|---|
| Our company (design, development, and installation) <br> Our company <u>has designed, developed,</u> and <u>installed.</u> . . . | Our company has done design, development, and installation of many display consoles. <br><br> (Three potential verbs.) |
| The beam (focusing) <br> The beam <u>is focused</u> by moving the. . . . (or: Focus the beam) | *Focusing* of <u>the beam</u> *is done* by moving the ring magnet along the axis of the tube. |
| The module (removal) <br> The module <u>is removed</u> by loosening the. . . . (or: Remove the) | Removal of <u>the module</u> is done by loosening the two hold-down screws and pulling on the module. |
| . . . . <u>carriers</u> (injection) <br> . . . . <u>carriers were injected</u> electrically | In Dr. Stubblefield's research, *injection* of <u>carriers</u> *was done* electrically. |

## 5-6  Review

Note while reviewing each frame how these changes continue the removal of deadwood: they always take out the weak verb and often function words, such as "the," "a," "of," "to," and "in." Consider how "made the preparation of" shortens to "prepared."

### *DEVELOP DYNAMIC VERBS*

| | |
|---|---|
| These efficiencies (dependent) <br> These <u>efficiencies</u> <u>depend</u> on the . . . . | These efficiencies are dependent on the minority-carrier lifetime. |
| this logic (operation) <br> This logic <u>operates</u> independently of the. . . . | The operation of this logic is independent of delay in the components. (Use "independently.") |
| This detector (use) <br> This detector <u>uses</u> the junction edge-on. . . . | This detector makes use of the junction edge-on to reduce sensitivity to variations. |
| These weights (excess) <br> These weights <u>exceed</u> those specified. | These weights *are in excess of* those specified. |
| Film-thickness (measurements) <br> Film thickness <u>is measured</u> with a . . . and a. . . . | Film-thickness measurements are done with a polarization interferometer and a multiple-beam interferometer. |

| | |
|---|---|
| the intensity of the . . . must (change) <br> The intensity of the . . . must change more rapidly. | The change in the intensity of the magnetic field must be more rapid. <br><br> The intensity of . . . must |
| This technical proposal (response) <br> This technical proposal responds to the. . . . | This technical proposal *is in response to* the Request for Quotation for "A Study of Bistable-element Switching." |
| He (design) <br> He designed transmission-preparation equipment. | He did design of transmission-preparation equipment. |
| His report (appraisal) <br> His report extensively appraised future. . . . | His report *made an* extensive *appraisal of* future space efforts. |
| Negative material (loss) <br> Negative material is rarely lost. | *Loss* of negative material *is* rare. |
| Mr. H. Randall (supervision) <br> Mr. H. Randall supervised the . . . | Mr. H. Randall did the assembly depart- and testing department supervision. |
| Resistance (measurements) <br> Resistance was measured during the. . . . | Resistance measurements were made during the annealing. <br> (Keep the tense past.) |
| The following (description) <br> The following describes. . . . | The following is a description of how it develops the gating voltages. |
| The . . . electrons (dependent) <br> The . . . electrons depends on. . . . | The number of electrons is dependent on the voltage. |
| The . . . components (limiting) <br> The . . . components limit the size. | The electronic components are size-limiting. |

COMMENT: NOT EVERY POTENTIAL VERB SHOULD BE TURNED INTO A VERB. SOME POSSIBLE CHANGES GIVE A DIFFERENT MEANING, AS DO THE FOLLOWING:

1. *Obtain an estimate of* (Estimate) the static weight.

THE REVISED SENTENCE DEMANDS THAT THE PERSON ADDRESSED DO THE ESTIMATING, WHICH IS NOT WHAT THE ORIGINAL CALLED FOR.

2. The voltage control *provides efficient operation* (operates efficiently) by adjusting the voltage.

THE ORIGINAL MAKES NO CLAIM ABOUT THE VOLTAGE CONTROL OPERATING EFFICIENTLY, JUST THAT IT BROUGHT ABOUT EFFICIENT OPERATION.

3. A reflective surface around a tube *equals an increase in* (increases) the area of the photocathode in the tube.

**A REFLECTIVE SURFACE AROUND A TUBE MAY BE EQUAL TO AN INCREASE IN THE AREA OF AN ELEMENT INSIDE THE TUBE, BUT IT CANNOT INCREASE THE SIZE OF THAT ELEMENT.**

4. The director *dares to differ* (differs) with the owner.

**THIS WOULD BE ACCEPTABLE ONLY IF THE ORIGINAL SENTENCE CARRIED THE WRONG MEANING.**
   **THE FOLLOWING CHANGES *MIGHT* GO TOO FAR:**

1. Shaded areas *will be devoted to manufacturing* (will manufacture) the escape locks.

**SINCE "AREAS" DON'T MANUFACTURE, A PASSIVE CONSTRUCTION MIGHT BE BETTER:**

The escape locks will be manufactured in the shaded areas.

2. Incorrect wiring *caused damage to* (damaged) the circuit.

**WIRING COULD AT MOST BE A FACTOR HELPING TO CAUSE THE DAMAGE.**

3. Rifle-drilled holes *provide lubrication to* (lubricate) both crankshaft and camshaft.

**OIL LUBRICATES; HOLES DO NOT.**
   **ALWAYS REVIEW REVISIONS TO BE SURE YOU RETAIN THE INTENDED MEANING.**

# OTHER WEAK VERBS

## 6-1   Verbs of Service: "Use," "Aid," "Serve"

Verbs such as "use" do little more than hint at activity while stifling potentially dynamic verbs, as in:

A flow of oxygen will be used over the growth zone.

"Flow" as a verb would be more descriptive:

"Oxygen will flow (be flowing) over the growth zone."

The following sentences rely on similar "verbs of service," verbs like "serve," "aid," and "employ." The upper left in each frame continues to give the subject and potential new verb. Look here for guidance if you run into difficulties. Single underlines in problem sentences indicate new subjects. Italics identify the verbs. Continue to review each frame before leaving it.

### REWRITE WITH DYNAMIC VERBS

| | |
|---|---|
| A signal generator (develop)<br>A signal generator develops the. . . . | A signal generator *is used to develop* the test signals. |
| Section 2.2 (description)<br>Section 2.2 describes nonlinear. | Section 2.2 *is devoted to a description* of nonlinear processing. |

. . .

| | |
|---|---|
| The . . . signals (monitor)<br>The fault-locating signals <u>monitor</u><br>the. . . . | The fault-locating signals *serve to monitor* the high-voltage interlock system. |
| Simplifying the layout (ease)<br>Simplifying the layout <u>will ease</u><br>production. | Simplifying the layout will conduce to ease production. |

COMMENT: THE NEW VERB IN THE PRECEDING FRAME CAME FROM AN INFINITIVE, "TO EASE." INFINITIVES ARE THE "TO" FORM OF VERBS, AS IN "TO DISTRIBUTE," "TO READ," AND "TO MEASURE." LIKE "-ION" AND "-ENT" WORDS, INFINITIVES OFTEN ARE POTENTIALLY VIGOROUS VERBS.

| | |
|---|---|
| [You] (observe) (an infinitive)<br><u>Observe</u> the waveforms on the. . . . | Use the oscilloscope to observe the waveforms.<br>_____ the waveforms on the . . .<br>(The subject is "you," understood.) |
| The AGC detector and amplifier (maintain) (an infinitive)<br>The AGC detector and amplifier <u>maintain</u> a constant. . . . | The AGC detector and amplifier operate to maintain a constant output from the I-F amplifier. |
| The control circuit (distribute)<br>The control circuit <u>distributes</u> the. . . . | The control circuit is employed to distribute the four input voltages. |
| The . . . processor (controller)<br>The input-output processor <u>con-</u><br><u>trols</u> communications. | The input-output processor *acts as a* communications *controller*. |
| Register senders (accumulate)<br>Register senders <u>accumulate</u> data until. . . . | Register senders *serve to accumulate* data until they can be processed. |
| The first wafer (control)<br>The first wafer <u>controls</u> the. . . . | The first wafer is used to control the input voltage. |

## 6-2   Verbs of Performance: "Perform," "Carry Out," "Conduct"

The weak verbs in the following frames can be called "verbs of performance," words like "perform," "carry out," and "conduct." They suggest the carrying on of an activity, as in:

The facilities engineering <u>department</u> <u>has performed</u> the *installation of* (has installed) the partitions.

## REWRITE WITH DYNAMIC VERBS

| | |
|---|---|
| The data analysis department (programming) <br> The <u>data analysis department</u> <u>pro-grams</u> for. . . . | The <u>data analysis department</u> *performs the programming* for our department. |
| The production department (typed) <br> The <u>production department</u> <u>types</u> the masters. | The production department *prepares the typed* masters. |
| We (study) <br> We <u>will</u> <u>study</u> the new. . . . | We will conduct a study of the new machines. |
| The limiter (remove) <br> The limiter <u>removes</u> residual. . . . | The limiter operates to remove residual amplitude modulation. |
| For this study <u>we</u> (generation) <br> For this study <u>we</u> <u>generated</u> simulated. . . . | For this study <u>we</u> *carried out generation of* simulated Raman emission in benzene. |
| The temperature of the. . . . <br> (change) <br> The temperature . . . <u>was</u> <u>changed</u> by. . . . | *A change in* the temperature of the cesium vapor *was obtained* by placing the bulb in water. |
| (you) (inspection) <br> <u>Inspect</u> periodically. | *Conduct inspections* periodically. <br> (Subject is "you," understood.) |
| The decoders (conversions) <br> The decoders <u>convert</u> signals from. . . . | The decoders perform conversions of signals from digital to analog. |

## 6-3  Verbs of Result: "Result In," "Obtain," "Yield"

Neutral verbs such as "result," "obtain," and "produce" often stifle straightforward statements about increases or decreases. In the following sentence the vagueness of "results" evades the stark fact of the decrease:

<u>Eliminating</u> speech redundancy <u>results</u> *in a decrease in* **(decreases) the required channel capacity.**

## REWRITE WITH DYNAMIC VERBS

| | |
|---|---|
| This change (simplification) <br> <s>This change simplifies the struc-ture.</s> | This change *results in simplification* of the structure. |

| | |
|---|---|
| The . . . sensors (interaction)<br>The sensors <u>must interact</u> minimally with. . . . | The dynamic-weight sensors must produce minimal interaction with traffic.<br><br>The . . . sensors must _____ minimally with. . . . |
| The . . . ratio (improvement)<br>The . . . <u>ratio</u> does not <u>improve</u>. | No improvement in the channel signal-to-noise ratio is obtained.<br><br>The channel . . . ratio does not |
| Changing . . . (reversal)<br>Changing the . . . field <u>can reverse</u> the direction. | Changing the intensity of the aligning field *can produce reversal of* the direction.<br><br>Changing the . . . can |
| This mass on the crystal (shift)<br><u>This mass</u> on the crystal slightly <u>shifts</u> the. . . . | This mass on the crystal *produces a* slight *shift in* the resonant frequency.<br><br>This mass on the . . . slightly |
| Incorporating (reducing)<br><u>Incorporating</u> these struts <u>can</u> also <u>reduce</u> the cost. | Incorporating these struts *can* also *result in reducing* the cost. |
| . . . noise (control)<br>Out-of-band <u>noise</u> <u>controls</u>. . . | Control for the combining is derived from <u>out-of-band noise</u>. |

## 6-4  Verbs of Giving: "Give," "Furnish," "Provide"

The weak verbs in this unit can be called "verbs of giving." They are verbs like "give," "furnish," and "provide," as in:

The transistor <u>stage</u> then <u>provides</u> *detection and amplification of* (**detects and amplifies**) the received signal.

Rewrite the following sentences with stronger verbs. Continue to review each frame.

### *REWRITE WITH DYNAMIC VERBS*

| | |
|---|---|
| [You] (circulation)<br>Gently <u>circulate</u> the. . . . | Provide gentle circulation of the oxalic acid during this period.<br><br>Gently _____ the oxalic acid. |
| The proposed design (satisfaction)<br><u>The</u> proposed <u>design</u> <u>will not satisfy</u> all. . . . | The proposed design will not give satisfaction of all the requirements. |

OTHER WEAK VERBS 65

| | |
|---|---|
| More complex problems (challenge)<br><u>More complex problems chal-<br>lenge</u> the. . . . | More complex problems present a challenge to the bright engineer. |
| Phase locking (improvement)<br><u>Phase locking can improve</u> (improves) the. . . . | Phase locking can furnish an improvement in the threshold level. |
| The cabinet (shielding)<br><u>The cabinet shields</u> against. . . . | The cabinet provides shielding against radio interference. |
| Two gas boilers (heat)<br><u>Two gas boilers heat</u> the building. | Two gas boilers supply heat to the building. |
| He (fly and maintain)<br><u>He will fly and maintain</u> both. . . . | He will be assigned to fly and maintain both planes. |
| the plots (discussion)<br><u>The plots were discussed</u> in. . . .<br>(or: The first report discussed. . . .) | A discussion of the plots was presented in the first report. |
| The . . . system (processing)<br><u>The . . . system</u> automatically and rapidly <u>processes</u> all. . . . | The automatic processing system *provides* automatic and rapid *processing of* all program runs and changes. |
| Also [you] (consideration)<br>Also <u>consider</u> alternatives. | Also *give consideration to* alternatives.<br><br>Also |
| These design criteria (limit)<br><u>These design criteria limit</u> the area of. . . . | These design criteria *place a limit* on the area of the diode. |
| This type of construction (provision)<br><u>This</u> . . . construction <u>provides</u> vides for simplifying (simplifies) overhauls. | This type of construction *makes provision for simplifying* overhauls. |
| Value engineering (spotlight)<br><u>Value engineering spotlights</u> factors that. . . . | Value engineering *puts the spotlight on* factors that increase the cost. |
| control (transfer)<br><u>Control is transferred</u> (transfers) automatically. . . . | Transfer of control to alternate consoles is provided automatically.<br><br>Control |
| The readout (identity)<br><u>The readout identifies</u> the. . . . | The readout shows the equipment identity. |

## 6-5   Verbs of Accomplishment: "Accomplish," "Cause," "Effect"

The nondynamic verbs in this section can be called "verbs of accomplishment." They are verbs like "accomplish" and "cause" and "effect," as in:

Erasing of any channel can be accomplished.

which can be rewritten:

Any channel can be erased.

A similar change can be made in sentences such as:

The phase transition causes *a change in* (changes) the birefringence.

## *REWRITE WITH DYNAMIC VERBS*

| | |
|---|---|
| We (inhibited) <br> We have adequately inhibited corrosion. | We have achieved adequate inhibition of corrosion. <br> We have adequately |
| The punch (cracking) <br> The punch might crack the board between. . . . | The punch *might cause cracking of* the board between closely spaced holes. |
| These logic circuits (transfer) <br> These logic circuits transfer the data. | These logic circuits effect the transfer of the data. |
| These sections (design) <br> These sections have been designed. | The design of these sections has been completed. |
| Speed (change) <br> Speed is changed by. . . . | Speed *change is accomplished* by an electric clutch. |
| This problem (solution) <br> This problem can be solved by. . . . | *A solution of* this problem *can be realized* by using a voice-excited vocoder. |
| The power-level (adjustments) <br> The power level is adjusted by. . . . | The power-level *adjustments are accomplished* by changing the beam voltage. |
| Operation (improved) <br> Operation (was) improved in July. | Improved operation was obtained in July. |

| | |
|---|---|
| Germanium substrates (limitations) <br> Germanium substrates <u>limit</u> deposition temperatures. . . . | Germanium substrates *impose limitations on* deposition temperatures of systems containing arsenic. |
| The idling signal (synchronism) <br> The idling signal <u>synchronizes</u> the oscillator. | The idling signal *maintains synchronism* of the oscillator. |

## 6-6   Verbs of Occurrence: "Occur," "Take Place," "Become"

The weak verbs in this section are verbs of occurrence, or happening, as in:

**Damage <u>occurred</u> to letters at four places along their path of travel.**

"Damage" explicitly pictures what "occurred" only hints at:

**Letters <u>were damaged</u> at four places along their path of travel.**

## REWRITE WITH DYNAMIC VERBS

| | |
|---|---|
| The lead dioxide coating (change) <br> The lead dioxide <u>coating changes</u> in volume. . . . | The lead dioxide coating *undergoes a change in* volume while charging and discharging. |
| A high-vacuum <u>pump</u> (failure) <br> A high-vacuum <u>pump failed</u> at the. . . . | A high-vacuum pump *failure occurred* at the beginning of the tests. |
| The data (transfer) <br> The data <u>transfer</u> through a. . . . | The data *transfer takes place* through a magnetic drum. |
| . . . the drive motor (stop) <br> . . . that <u>the drive motor stops</u> completely before. . . . | The new coupling ensures that <u>the drive motor</u> *comes to a* complete *stop* before it can be restarted. |
| . . . if a fault (causes) <br> . . . if a <u>fault causes</u> removal of (removes) the. . . . | The indicator will light if a fault *occurs which causes* removal of the beam voltage. |

## 6-7   Verbs of Possession: "Have," "Possess," "Belong"

The following sentences rely on weak "verbs of possession." Forms of "have" predominate, as in:

The new template <u>has</u> resemblance to (resembles) the old one.

## REWRITE WITH DYNAMIC VERBS

| | |
|---|---|
| Figure 7 (listing)<br>Figure 7 <u>lists</u> all power. . . . | Figure 7 includes a listing of all power out-puts at full load. |
| The . . . equipment (interaction)<br>The . . . equipment <u>should inter-act</u> as little as. . . . | The data-collection equipment should have as little interaction as possible with traffic flow. |
| Section I (illustrations and de-scriptions)<br>Section I <u>illustrates and describes</u> all. . . . | Section I contains illustrations and descrip-tions of all operating and power controls. |
| Cell temperature (affects)<br>Cell temperature <u>affects</u> the. . . . | Cell temperature has an effect on the charging voltage.<br><br>("Effect" becomes "affects.") |
| The card reader (reading)<br>The card reader <u>reads</u> (at a rate of) 2,000 cards a minute. | The card reader *has a reading* rate of 2,000 cards a minute.<br><br>("Rate of" can become superfluous.) |
| The conversion (addition)<br>The conversion <u>adds</u> two receivers and. . . . | The conversion *involves the addition of* two receivers and one antenna at each terminal. |
| The . . . typewriter (communi-cating)<br>The console typewriter <u>communi-cates</u> directly with the. . . . | The console typewriter *has the function of communicating* directly with the central proc-essor. ("Function" becomes superfluous.) |

## 6-8   Other Weak Verbs

Here are weak verbs that don't fit in the preceding groups.

## REWRITE WITH DYNAMIC VERBS

| | |
|---|---|
| The C. Haggerty Corporation (study and use)<br>The C. Haggerty Corporation <u>has been studying and using</u> phase-lock devices. . . . | The C. Haggerty Corporation *has been en-gaged in the study and the use of* phase-lock devices since 1938. |
| TIVAK (conversion)<br>TIVAK <u>converts</u> these data. | TIVAK *handles* this data *conversion*. |

| | |
|---|---|
| The reflective coating (double)<br>The reflective coating almost dou-<br>bles the light-gathering efficiency. | The reflective coating *increases* the light-gathering efficiency *by almost double.* |
| The . . . pump (replacement)<br>The high-vacuum pump was re-<br>placed. | The high-vacuum pump *replacement was installed.* |
| . . . discussion (considering)<br>. . . the discussion considers only<br>twofold combining. | For simplicity, the discussion *is limited to considering* only twofold combining. |
| The central controller (establish)<br>The central controller establishes<br>the. . . . | The central controller proceeds to establish the connection. |
| Our department (recommenda-<br>tions)<br>Our department then recommends<br>how to. . . . | Our department then *submits recommendations on* how to eliminate the expense. |
| This department (providing)<br>This department is providing (pro-<br>vides) technical services to . . . | This department is engaged in providing technical services to the government. |

## 6-9  Review

Only a few of the sentences at the lower left have underlines. However, when you check there and when reviewing, concentrate on the change in subject and verb.

### REWRITE WITH DYNAMIC VERBS

| | |
|---|---|
| The main blower (cooling)<br>The main blower cools the iron-<br>core components. . . . | The main blower provides cooling of the iron-core components and the silicon rectifier. |
| This temperature change (in-<br>crease)<br>This temperature change should<br>have increased the . . . pressure. | This temperature change *should have produced an increase in* the cesium vapor pressure. |
| Electron backscattering (limita-<br>tions)<br>Electron backscattering seriously<br>limits collection of. . . . | Electron backscattering *presents* a serious *limitation to* collection of high-energy carriers. |
| This pulse (blank)<br>This pulse blanks the CRT display. | This pulse is used to blank the CRT display. |

| | |
|---|---|
| Their army (transportation) <br> Their army cannot transport our equipment. | Their army cannot furnish transportation for our equipment. |
| Normally, one air conditioner (maintain) <br> Normally, one air conditioner maintains the temperature and. . . . | Normally, one air conditioner operates to maintain the temperature and humidity listed below. |
| our scientists (treatment) <br> Our scientists have treated this problem mathematically. | The mathematical treatment of this problem has been carried out by <u>our scientists.</u> (Rewrite in active voice.) |
| You (check) <br> <u>Do not check</u> the voltage with an ammeter. | Do not use an ammeter to check the voltage. <br><br> Do not _____ with. . . . |
| the output (deterioration) <br> The output deteriorates rapidly. | A deterioration of the output occurs rapidly. |
| Time-delay relays (delay) <br> Time-delay relays delay contact with. . . . | Time-delay relays are employed to delay contact with the pressure plates. |
| The weight reduction (increased) <br> The weight reduction will increase production costs. | The weight reduction *will result in increased* production costs. |
| Dr. J. P. McCarthy (analysis) <br> Dr. J. P. McCarthy analyzed several. . . . | Dr. J. P. McCarthy conducted an analysis of several collection techniques. |
| These toxic substances (damage) <br> The toxic substances damage the liver far less than. . . . | These toxic substances *produce* far less liver *damage* than those mentioned above. |
| A series of . . . (monitor) <br> A series of signal lights monitors the. . . . | A series of signal lights serves to monitor the interlocks. |
| This . . . system (reductions) <br> This speech-compression system reduces bandwidth by ten to one. | This speech-compression system *obtains* bandwidth *reductions* of ten to one. |
| The primary winding (rejection) <br> The primary winding rejects the carrier frequency. | The primary winding provides rejection of the carrier frequency. |
| This (load) <br> This loads the motor. | This puts a load on the motor. |

| | |
|---|---|
| The . . . transport (couple)<br>The magnetic tape transport couples the speech analyzer. . . . | The magnetic-tape transport is used to couple the speech analyzer to a card punch. |
| Sediment accumulation (solution)<br>Sediment accumulation will eventually solve these. . . . | Sediment accumulation will eventually provide a solution to these problems. |
| The absorption level (change)<br>The absorption level changes immediately. | *The change in* the absorption level *occurs* immediately. |
| This component (switching)<br>This component automatically switches. . . . | This component *performs* automatic *switching* if commercial power fails. |
| Infrared . . . measurements . . . substrate (confirm)<br>. . . measurements of . . . confirm the identity. | Infrared-transmission measurements of films on a transparent substrate *give confirmation of* the identity. |
| This (reduction)<br>This can further reduce the. . . . | This can result in a further reduction in the number of gaps.<br><br>This can further |
| Its electrical . . . capability (study)<br>Its electrical recharging capability will be studied. | *A study of* its electrical recharging capability *will be performed.* |
| Our representatives (establishing)<br>Our representatives have been establishing engineering. . . . | Our representatives have been engaged in establishing engineering depots in foreign countries. |
| A . . . stage (amplify)<br>A . . . stage amplifies the. . . . | A transistor stage is used to amplify the intercom signal. |
| the adapter ring (installed)<br>The adapter ring was installed in November. | *Installation* of the adapter ring was *accomplished* in November. |
| the program (interruption)<br>The program is interrupted when a word. . . . | An interruption in the program occurs when a word is transferred. |
| The gauge (calibration)<br>The gauge has not been calibrated yet. | Calibration of the gauge has not yet been accomplished. |

Experienced listeners (averages)
Experienced listeners consistently averaged higher than. . . .

Experienced listeners consistently *had* higher *averages* than inexperienced listeners.

size (reduction)
The size was reduced twenty to one (one-twentieth).

A size *reduction* of twenty to one *was achieved*.

The size was

Section 2 (discussion)
Section 2 discusses the shear zones in more detail.

Section 2 contains a more detailed discussion of the shear zones.

injection lasers (development)
Injection lasers have (been) developed to the point where. . . .

*The development of* injection lasers *has progressed* to the point where red or near infrared can be produced.

Weight (reductions)
Weight can be reduced only by reducing the density.

Weight reduction can be accomplished only by reducing the density.

This circuit (increasing)
This circuit increases the. . . .

This circuit has the effect of increasing the amplitude of small signals.

("The effect of" becomes superfluous.)

. . . the operator (routing)
In the dc patch bay the operator can route messages over. . . .

In the dc patch bay the operator *can effect routing of* messages over alternate circuits.

Opening the (activate)
Opening the front panel activates the safety switch.

Opening the front panel *causes* the safety switch *to activate*.

We (diagram)
We have diagramed that circuit.

We *have completed a diagram of* that circuit.

. . . optical transmission (measurements)
Optical transmission was also measured.

*Measurements* were also *taken of* optical transmission.

Our department (studying)
Our department has been studying the practicability of. . . .

Our department has been engaged in studying the practicability of active metal-air batteries.

The heating (breakup)
The heating breaks up the. . . .

The heating accomplishes the breakup of the chemical bond.

# DEVELOPING OTHER VERB FORMS

We have been strengthening the main sentence verb. Now we will turn elsewhere in the sentence, developing verbs, infinitives, and gerunds—all of which are more lively than nouns.

## 7-1  Verbs in Dependent Clauses

The following is an independent clause:

**"Send the beginning-of-message word."**

It is a clause because it has a subject ("you" is understood) and because it has a verb. It is independent because it can stand alone. Independent clauses are the core of sentences. Other elements often supplement them, as in:

**Send the beginning-of-message word** *before transmitting the text.*

Sometimes it is desirable to develop verbs in this supplementary material, for example:

**Send the . . .** *before you transmit the text.*

The supplementary material is now a dependent clause—a clause because of its subject and verb, dependent because it is incomplete: standing alone, it does not carry meaning.

You will be developing dependent clauses in the following problem sentences.

Do not touch the independent clause (the main subject and its verb). Expressions to be revised are sometimes in italics.

## DEVELOP DEPENDENT CLAUSES

| | |
|---|---|
| Because it is (has been) used in surface-barrier. . . . | Because *of its use* in surface-barrier transistors, this type of interface has been thoroughly studied.<br><br>Because it is \_\_\_\_\_ in surface-barrier. . . . |
| . . . because funds were (are) limited. | We could not develop a reliable and economical method of classifying data because of the limitation of funds.<br><br>. . . because funds |

In addition to the benefits of verbs in place of abstract nouns, dependent clauses often show relationships of ideas more precisely. They often call for a subordinating conjunction whose meaning was not originally present. For example, to change the sentence:

**This publication discusses the construction of subscriber terminals.**

To change this so that it has a dependent clause you have to use one of the following subordinating conjunctions:

**This publication discusses (how, where, when, why, which, what) subscriber terminals were constructed.**

Use the subordinating conjunctions given with the following sentences.

## DEVELOP DEPENDENT CLAUSES

| | |
|---|---|
| . . . in the area that you intend to activate the. . . . | Notify everyone in the area of your intention to activate the circuits.<br><br>. . . in the area *that* you \_\_\_\_\_ to activate the. . . . |
| Check that all boards are securely mounted. | Check all boards for secure mounting.<br><br>Check *that* \_\_\_\_\_ are securely |
| . . . while the first instruction is (being) executed. | The input must be available during the execution of the first instruction.<br><br>. . . must be available *while* \_\_\_\_\_ is being |

| ... on films that have the. ... | We will finish our study with measurements on films having the compositions listed below. |
| | ... on films that _____ the compositions listed below. |
| ... explains how the tuning method was selected. | This section explains selection of the tuning method. |
| | ... explains how _____ was |
| advantage that it needs less drive power. | This circuit has the additional advantage of needing less drive power. |
| | ... advantage that it _____ less drive power. |
| When power is applied, . . . . | Upon application of power, dangerous voltages build up. |
| | When power _____, dangerous voltages. . . . |
| ... a theory of how these devices operate. | Our engineers have also developed a theory of the operation of these devices. |
| | ... a theory of how |
| ... explains how citations are retrieved. | This section explains the retrieval of citations. |
| | ... explains how |

## 7-2 Infinitives from Nouns

Nouns in the following problem sentences cannot become verbs. But you can change them into infinitives, the "to" form of verbs, which are more action-oriented than are nouns. Thus

**For alignment of (To align) the tuner, first switch the power off.**

The upper left in the following frames gives the potential infinitive.

### CHANGE NOUNS INTO INFINITIVES

| (appearance) _____ causes fractures to appear. (. . . . . . causes fractures.) | This arcing causes *the appearance of* fractures. |
| | ... causes fractures to |

| (reduction) | Efficient encoding of speech promises *a significant reduction in* bit rate. |
| . . . promises to reduce the bit rate significantly. | . . . promises to _____ the bit rate significantly. |
| (agreement) | Our results appear in agreement with Clegg's. |
| . . . appear to agree with Clegg's. | . . . appear to |
| (redesign) | We will begin *redesign of* the prototype mail handler. |
| We will begin to redesign the prototype. . . . | We will begin to. . . . |
| (completion) | We need the airplane for the efficient completion of this project. |
| . . . *to* complete this project efficiently. | . . . the airplane to. . . . |
| (alignment) (adjustment) | The tables that follow contain all the information needed for alignment and adjustment of the radio. |
| needed to align and adjust the. . . . | |
| (detection) | *For satellite detection,* the set must survey each range for a number of cycles, depending on the doppler frequency. |
| To detect satellites, the set. . . . | |
| (reaching) | *For reaching* the couplers, remove the following plates. |
| To reach the couplers, . . . . | |

Sometimes you can replace weak infinitives with more dynamic ones, as in:

**We had enough time** *to perform comparisons* **(to compare) three soil samples.**

Develop similar infinitives in the following sentences.

## REWRITE WITH NEW INFINITIVES

| (alignment) of | *To achieve alignment of* the L-C section use a plastic screwdriver. |
| To align the L-C section. . . . | |
| (routing, testing, evaluating) | Its instruments are used *for routing, testing, and evaluating* the audio lines. |
| are used to route, test, and evaluate the audio lines. | |
| (reading) | *To obtain an* accurate *reading of* specific gravity, allow time for the acid to diffuse around the plates. |
| To read the specific gravity accurately. . . . | |
| (stabilization) | Allow five minutes for the oscillator stabilization. |
| . . . for the oscillator to stabilize | |

| (interpretation) | They refused to supply an interpretation of the strains. |
| They refused to interpret the strains. | |

| (evaluation) | Calibrate often enough to ensure adequate evaluation of the set. |
| Calibrate often enough to evaluate the set adequately. | |

## 7-3 Gerunds from Nouns

You can change some nouns that cannot become verbs or infinitives into gerunds, the "-ing" form of verbs. For example:

**"The prepara**tion **of proposals" can become "Prepar**ing **proposals."**

**"Proposal prepara**tion**" too can become "Prepar**ing **proposals."**

The "-ion" endings change into "-ing" endings. These are gerunds, which, though still nouns, are more dynamic because they are closer to their verb origin than are the other noun forms. Gerunds emphasize the activity role; most other nouns emphasize the naming.

Potential gerunds in the following sentences are in patterns such as "the . . . -ion of" and "an . . . -ion of." If you run into difficulty, upper left gives the potential gerund.

## CHANGE NOUNS TO GERUNDS—"-ING" FORMS

| (addition) | Our technicians corrected this fault by *the addition of* a jet at the lower surface of the input hopper. |
| by adding a jet at the. . . . | |

| (elimination) | *The elimination of* long runs will reduce special programming. |
| Eliminating long runs | |

| (replacement) | This problem was eliminated by *the replacement of* the stop roller with a stop spring. |
| by replacing the stop roller. . . . | |

| (fabrication) | Mating the semiconductor film onto the base is the most significant aspect in the fabrication of metal-base transistors. |
| . . . aspect in fabricating metal-base transistors. | |

| (Collection and classification) | We have to discover reliable, economical, and automatic instruments for *the collection and classification of* traffic data. |
| for collecting and classifying traffic data. | |

| (adjustment) | This design does not include potentiometers |
| --- | --- |
| . . . for adjusting the output voltage. | for the adjustment of the output voltage. |

The potential gerunds in the following sentences are in similar patterns. But in some, "the," "a," or "an" is missing.

| (selection) | This can be done by *selection of* the correct |
| --- | --- |
| . . . by selecting the correct pinched gases. . . . | pinched gases, gas contaminants, and gas pressure. |
| (determination) | Doping levels were established by determination of the resistivity and the Hall coefficient. |
| . . . by determining the resistivity and the. . . . | |
| (elimination) | Elimination of a 2- or 3-millisecond segment |
| Eliminating a 2- or 3-millisecond. . . . | from the beginning of a word does not decrease intelligibility. |
| (Rotation) | Rotation of the crucible necessitates the following three changes: |
| Rotating the crucible . . . | |

You will have to recast the following sentences slightly.

| (synchronization) | These loops were used for the television re- |
| --- | --- |
| . . . for synchronizing the television receiver. | ceiver synchronization. |
| (operation) | A system proves its worth by reliable operation. |
| . . . by operating reliably. | |
| (reduction) | The major topic will be a delay-line storage |
| . . . for reducing frame-to-frame redundancy. | for *frame-to-frame–redundancy reduction*. |

In the following frames you will be developing more dynamic gerunds in place of weak ones.

| (assembled and set up) | During the past month we have concentrated |
| --- | --- |
| . . . on assembling and setting up equipment. | on *getting* equipment *assembled and set up*. |

| | |
|---|---|
| (distortions)<br>. . . by distorting the magnetic field. | We increased the response by *introducing* magnetic field *distortions*. |
| (coupled)<br>. . . by coupling an automatic switchboard with a. . . . | They satisfied these requirements by *installing* an automatic switchboard *coupled* with a sophisticated control center. |
| (use)<br>. . . while using D₂ radiation. | They sought radio-frequency resonances while *making use of* $D_2$ radiation. |

The potential "-ing" words in the following sentences do not have the usual "-ion," "ent," "-ity" endings.

| | |
|---|---|
| (studies)<br>In addition to studying the structure. . . . | In addition to *studies of* the structure, we measured the optical transmission. |
| (use)<br>. . . by using a. . . . | This problem has been overcome by *the use of* a new source of zinc sulfide. |
| (removal)<br>After removing the copper, . . . | After removal of the copper, immediately wash the circuit board in running tap water. |
| (change)<br>Changing the magnitude. . . . | *A change in* the magnitude of the aligning field reverses the direction. |

COMMENT: SOME VERB FORMS ARE GENERALLY PREFERABLE TO OTHERS. HERE IS ONE ORDER OF PREFERENCE, THE MOST PREFERABLE FIRST:

1. ACTIVE VOICE, PRESENT TENSE:

The technician adjusts the heat.

2. INFINITIVE:

Do the following to *adjust* the heat.

3. PASSIVE VOICE:

The heat *was adjusted* by the technician.

4. NOUN FORMS ENDING IN "-ING":

*Adjusting* the heat was easy.

5. NOUN FORMS ENDING IN "-ION," "-ENT," "ENCE," ETC.:

*The adjustment* of the heat was easy.

## 7-4 REVIEW

### Verbs

Using the linking word given in the frames, develop dependent clauses in the following sentences. Upper left gives the potential verb.

### DEVELOP DEPENDENT CLAUSES

| | |
|---|---|
| (provision)<br>. . . how temporary equipment is provided. | This supplement discusses the provision of temporary equipment.<br><br>. . . how temporary equipment is |
| (is)<br>. . . because it is simple and economical. | This method was selected because of its simplicity and economy.<br><br>. . . because it is |
| (compliance)<br>. . . that we are complying with high standards of workmanship. | The daily inspection of subassemblies will assure you of our compliance with high standards of workmanship.<br><br>. . . that we are |
| (change)<br>How capacitance changes with temperature. . . . | *The change of capacitance with temperature is now being studied.*<br><br>How capacitance _____ with temperature. . . . |
| (direction)<br>. . . transfer input signals as directed by an . . . | The input-switching circuits transfer input signals *under direction of* an automatic switching control.<br><br>. . . signals as _____ by an |
| (completion)<br>. . . when he completes the. . . . | He will take up his new duties on completion of the overseas project.<br><br>. . . when he |
| (shipment)<br>. . . when you ship the oxidizer. | Follow the instructions in force at the time of shipment of the oxidizer.<br><br>. . . in force when you |
| (installation)<br>. . . how the permanent subscriber terminals were installed. | This report explains the installation of permanent subscriber terminals.<br><br>. . . explains how _____ were |

| (having) | This signal produces a tape having its own routing. |
|---|---|
| . . . a tape that has its own routing. | . . . a tape that |

## Infinitives

Change nouns in the following sentences into infinitives:

| (agreement) | If the committee is not able *to reach an agreement* on an agenda, he will take over. |
|---|---|
| . . . is not able to agree on an agenda. . . . | |
| (comparison) | *To make a comparison of* these two systems, we equalized their dynamic ranges. |
| To compare these two. . . . | |
| (separation) | *To provide separation of* the beams, they have been polarized perpendicular to each other. |
| To separate the beams. . . . | |
| (dependent) | The temperature of the crystalline transitions was found *to be dependent* on the physical characteristics of the evaporated compound. |
| . . . was found to depend (depended) on the. . . . | |
| (routing, testing, and evaluating) | The audio test bay is a central location for instruments used to perform routing, testing, and evaluating of the audio-frequency lines. (There are three.) |
| . . . used to route, test, and evaluate the. . . . | |
| (applying) | We can have broader bandwidths if we are willing to pay the penalty of applying additional power. |
| . . . if we are willing to apply. . . . | |
| (operation) | This feature allows operation of the processor at any clock rate. |
| . . . allows the processor to operate at any. . . . | |
| (training) | That group was organized for the specific purpose of training programmers for our computers. ("Purpose of" becomes superfluous.) |
| . . . was organized specifically to train. . . . | |
| (operation) | The processor and the magnetic drum enable operation of the system continuously. |
| . . . enable the system to operate continuously. | . . . enable the system to |
| (reduction) | Techniques now being studied promise further reductions in the bit rate. |
| . . . promise to reduce the bit rate further. | . . . promise to _____ the bit rate further. |

| (evaporation) | For the evaporation of the GaAs films the temperature must range from 1200 to 1800°C. |
|---|---|
| To evaporate the GaAs films. . . . | |

| (operation) | These circuits will be redesigned for operation over a wider range of pitch, amplitude, and voice quality. |
|---|---|
| . . . redesigned to operate over a | |

| (alignment) | To achieve alignment of the tuner, first turn off the power. |
|---|---|
| To align the tuner. . . . | |

### Gerunds

Change nouns in the following sentences into "-ing" words (gerunds):

| (replacement) | The changeover is easily made by the replacement of the I-F strips. |
|---|---|
| . . . by replacing the I-F strips. | |

| (reduction) | This kind of structure increases the weight-*reduction* possibility. |
|---|---|
| . . . the possibility of reducing the weight. | |

| (use) | We also considered *the use of* optical pumping to detect audio-modulated radio frequencies. |
|---|---|
| . . . considered using optical pumping. . . . | |

| (interpretation) | Our study has led to new techniques for the interpretation of diffraction patterns of twinned deposits. |
|---|---|
| . . . for (of) interpreting diffraction patterns. . . . | |

| (injection, transport(ation), and collection) | This type of transistor achieves power gain by *the injection, transport, and collection of* hot electrons in the central metal film. |
|---|---|
| . . . by injecting, transporting, and collecting hot electrons. . . . | |

| (preparation) | Vacuum evaporation is widely used in *the preparation of* thin films. |
|---|---|
| . . . in preparing thin films. | |

| (documentation) | This record-keeping system will aid greatly in documentation of the system. |
|---|---|
| . . . in documenting the system. | |

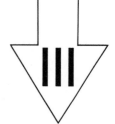

# USING
# LEAN WORDS

Use the simplest words adequate to carry your message. Long and weighty ones are not signs of literary skill; they often signify just the opposite. Weightier words carry extra meanings. Where simpler ones can do the job, the unnecessary meanings are semantic noise, that is, unnecessary information, which burdens the reader and often misleads him. He has to take in all the information; then, to get the intended meaning, he has to sieve out the excess—if he can. Literary expertise would save him this labor.

# LIGHTWEIGHT FUNCTION WORDS AND WORDS OF QUANTITY AND OF TIME

8

Function words such as "and," "if," and "of" carry little meaning. They serve primarily to develop relationships between other words. Yet, since they are about half the words written, ponderous ones disproportionately overload a style, as by using "in conjunction with" instead of "and" or "when it is the case that" instead of "if."

We have already seen that the vocabulary of technical writing has a high percentage of words of quantity and time. These too are often overweight, as in "a major portion of" used instead of "most." Where simple lightweight words would do, use them. You will considerably lighten your style and help your readers understand you.

## 8-1 Function Words

### "And"

The writers of the following sentences used overblown expressions such as "in conjunction with" and "as well as" in place of the simple word "and." Like "and," these expressions link other sentence elements, but they do more than "and": "in conjunction with" stresses the activity of joining or the state of being joined, which "and" does not do. "As well as" suggests an earlier reference to what follows it, again something "and" does not do. Where these additional meanings are relevant, those words should, of course, be used, but they should not be used merely as showy replacements for "and."

## REPLACE OVERWEIGHT EXPRESSIONS WITH "AND"

| You should have replaced: | Our engineers have developed the material technology as well as the fabrication techniques. |
| --- | --- |
| as well as | |
| along with | Passive filters along with microelectronics reduced its size and weight. |

COMMENT: IN REVIEWING THESE SENTENCES, COMPARE THE ORIGINAL WORD WITH ITS LIGHT-WEIGHT REPLACEMENT. NOTE THE INCREASED DIRECTNESS OF THE LEANER WORD.

| plus | The conversion adds new receivers plus quadruple diversity. |
| --- | --- |
| in conjunction with | We hope this data in conjunction with the I-V-T data will explain the unusual diode properties. |

### "Of"

The ponderous expressions in the following sentences include verbs ending in "-ed":

## REPLACE OVERWEIGHT EXPRESSIONS WITH "OF"

| realized from | The most important feature of this communications system was the quality and reliability *realized from* the voice and teletype circuits. |
| --- | --- |
| obtained from | The results obtained from these tests are satisfactory. |
| encountered in | These consoles can take the normal shock and vibration encountered in shipping. |

### "For"

The weighty expressions in the following sentences are infinitives:

## REPLACE INFINITIVES WITH "FOR"

| | |
|---|---|
| to achieve | To achieve high gain and phase inversion, transformer couple each stage. |
| To permit | To permit more reliable operation, we sealed the other vans against dust and rain. |
| To ensure | To ensure a secure fit use the smaller hole. |
| to perform | You need only 128 words to perform addition. |

The long expressions that "for" can replace in the following sentences are not infinitives:

| | |
|---|---|
| with respect to | Evaluate more promising systems *with respect to* speaker identification and naturalness of speech. |
| throughout | This problem will continue throughout the duration of the war. |
| in the case of | This is true only in the case of high-temperature deposition. |
| Pursuant to | Pursuant to contract BC 93-630, our plant delivered a 600-channel, range-gated processor. |

### "So"

Replace expressions in the following sentences with "so":

## REPLACE WEIGHTY EXPRESSIONS WITH "SO"

| | |
|---|---|
| in such a manner (that) | Align the tubes in such a manner that they all heat at the same time. |
| in order (that) | We use an oscillator-amplifier combination in order that the reflector surfaces will not be damaged. |
| in such a way (that) | Mount all equipment in such a way that no material or structural member experiences excessive shock. |

### "As" and "So As"

Replace the following italicized expressions with "as" or "so as." Then check left:

*INSERT "AS" OR "SO AS"*

| | |
|---|---|
| as (for) | Timing tracks contain prerecorded pulses used *to provide* timing signals. |
| as | Each matrix appears *in the form of* an alphabetic or a numeric character. |
| So as | In order not to complicate the logic circuits, we used the natural periods of the most significant digits in the binary codes. |

### "On" and "In"

Replace the italicized expressions with "on" or "in." Be sure to review each frame.

*REVISE WITH "ON" OR "IN"*

| | |
|---|---|
| on | Dirt or grease *adhering to* the float will change the specific-gravity reading. |
| in (by) | The contractor has access to all information uncovered *as a result of* this research. |
| on (about) | We have studied their comments *concerning* recent developments. |
| in | This technique is limited only *by the fact* that it reduces FM sidebands. |
| on (about) | They asked four questions *regarding* quality. |

### "By" and "With"

Replace long expressions in the following sentences with "by" or "with":

*REWRITE, USING "BY" OR "WITH"*

| | |
|---|---|
| by (with) | We reached this goal *via* support from government agencies. |

| with | Clean the relay contacts *by using* contact cleaner on a chamois stretched over a thin piece of wood or metal. |
| --- | --- |
| by | Films produced *using* this method have a wurtzite structure. |
| with | Correct the proof sheets *by means of* standard proofreader's marks. |
| by (or: "with a newly") | We overcame this problem *through* using a newly designed zinc sulfide source. |
| by (in) | The output of this filter is first amplified, then shaped *via* a Schmidt trigger circuit. |

### "If" or "Where" Instead of "In Case" and "In the Event"

Most of the long expressions in the following sentences are "in case" and "in the event."

*REWRITE WITH "IF" OR "WHERE"*

| If (When) | *In the event* an alarm lamp lights, troubleshoot as follows: . . . |
| --- | --- |
| If | *In case* the printer does not stop, press the following push buttons: . . . |
| If (When) | The assembly language can be modified *in the event that* requirements change. |
| Where (If) | *For those situations in which* stress distribution is a problem, we will install alarms. |

### New Verb When Replacing "In the Event Of"

You will have to develop new verbs for the following sentences. For example:

*In the event of* **equipment** *failure,* **turn off the main power.**

becomes:

*If* **the equipment** *fails,* **turn off the main power.**

## *REWRITE WITH "IF," DEVELOPING NEW VERBS WHERE NECESSARY*

| | |
|---|---|
| If a fuse blows, 48. . . . | *In the event of* a fuse blowing, 48 volts goes to the warning light. |
| If a single beam fails. . . . | *In the event of* a single beam failing, this can replace it. |
| If a vibrator malfunctions, notify. . . . | *In the case of* the vibrator malfunctioning, notify us immediately. |
| If (When) a high-priority message is delayed, . . . | *In the event of* a high-priority message being delayed, the warning light blinks. |

The following forms a short review:

## *REPLACE OVERLONG EXPRESSIONS WITH "AND," "OF," OR "FOR"*

| | |
|---|---|
| and | Each slide shows the timing pulse *together with* the detector pulse. |
| of | The conclusions *generated by* this study are listed below. |
| For | *To accomplish* this check, overlap the pulses. |
| For | *In the case of* each compound, the temperature of the substrates determined the crystalline structure. |
| and | The contractor arranged for interisland transportation, for delivery of trucks, *as well as* for air transportation. |

## 8-2  Quantity Words

### "Much," "Most," "Many," "More," "Some"

You can often replace overblown quantity expressions with simple words such as "most" and "many."

*A portion* (**Some**) **of this signal replaces.** . . .

Similarly, "a wide variety of" can become "many" or "many kinds of." "The bulk of" can become "most."

## REPLACE QUANTITY EXPRESSIONS WITH ONE OF THOSE SUGGESTED

| | |
|---|---|
| Most | We finished *the bulk* of the analysis in the first two weeks. |
| | some / most / more |
| many | The cleavage created *numerous* problems. |
| | other / many / some |
| many | These circuits have *numerous* connections. |
| | many / more / larger |
| more than | The "Return on Investment" column applies to items that cost *in excess of* $100,000. |
| | about / more than / approximately |
| much | The Wheatstone bridge is *considerably* smaller. |
| | much / a little / often |
| more | Parallel readers need *a larger number of* read amplifiers. |
| | many / much / more |
| most | Our laboratories already have *a major portion* of this equipment. |
| | most / considerable / quantities |
| much | We put *a great deal of* research into selecting the alloy. |
| | much / more than / many kinds of |

### Other Words

## REPLACE OVERWEIGHT QUANTITY EXPRESSIONS WITH ONE OF THOSE GIVEN

| | |
|---|---|
| enough | The electron penetration generated *sufficient quantities of* hole-electron pairs to absorb infrared radiation. |
| | enough / more / many |

| | |
|---|---|
| about (or: . . . will about triple the speed.) | Data processing will increase the speed *in the area of* three times. |
| | about / more than / less than. |
| all | Men listed in the red-coded area will put *100 percent* of their time on this project. |
| | all / most / more |
| We will also install | *In addition* we will install a display to handle the higher rates. |
| | then / also / first |

COMMENT: ESPECIALLY IN DIGITAL CONTEXTS, "IN ADDITION" CALLS TO MIND MATHEMATICAL OR LOGICAL ADDITION.

| | |
|---|---|
| about | The output of this system should be *in the range of* 12,000 bits a second. |
| | less than / about / more than |
| greater than | These quantities are *in excess of* those listed. |
| | approximately / often / greater than |
| also (We *also* have to) | *In addition* we have to install a gear that meshes with the output gear. |
| | also / soon / afterward |
| enough | He will still have a *sufficient quantity of* attitude-control gas. |
| | more / enough / too much |

### "-Est" Words Instead of Expressions Such as "Maximum" and "Minimum"

"Optimum," "maximum," and "minimum" are misused so often that they should be avoided. "Optimum," for example, refers to the product of conflicting factors; it does not mean "best." If you mean "best," write "best," and if you mean best in some way, say in what way. "Maximum" and "minimum" can often be replaced by "-est" words, such as "longest," "biggest," "greatest," "smallest," and "least."

## INSERT SIMPLER REPLACEMENTS

| | |
|---|---|
| at least | Their local-oscillator frequencies differ by *a minimum of* 50 megacycles. |
| | at least / at most / about |
| better | Black mentioned another method that yields slightly *more optimum* results. |
| | better / higher / lower |
| as much as possible (most) | The time constant must be large enough that the receiver rejects *the maximum* of the signal interference. |
| | all / as much as possible / some |
| smallest (the smallest hole) | For the most secure connection use the *minimum size* hole. |
| | lowest / least / smallest |
| best | I made this value a variable to help in finding the *optimum* value. |
| | highest / best / lowest |
| as much as (where) | We will use standard parts *to the maximum extent* possible. |
| | as much as (where) / not / always |

## 8-3   Time Words

Many time references use overweight terms, for example, "preliminary" and "initial" instead of "first," "subsequent" instead of "later," and "prior" instead of "before."

## INSERT SIMPLER TIME EXPRESSIONS

| | |
|---|---|
| before | He improved the mail handler *prior to* the final test. |
| | with / before / at |

| | |
|---|---|
| during | Our present program will continue *concurrently with* the proposed program. |
| | following / during / within |
| when necessary | We will review these recommendations *as the occasion warrants.* |
| | soon / later / when necessary |
| before | The first word is repeated at the end of the loading cycle and *prior to* transmitting the text. |
| | after / during / before |
| at the same time (together) | Have them all heat *simultaneously.* |
| | at the same time / quickly / later |
| first (early) | For this reason, we made the *initial* structures with Ag films. |
| | first / present / future |
| now | Our company is *currently* sponsoring basic speech studies. |
| | still / first / now |
| now | *At present* we are calculating the photocurrent delivered by the new diodes. |
| | still / now / sometimes |

COMMENT: "TIMELY" DOES NOT MEAN "ON TIME." "A TIMELY ARRIVAL" IS AN "OPPORTUNE," "WELL-TIMED," OR "SEASONABLE" ARRIVAL, NOT AN "ON-TIME" ARRIVAL. "PRESENTLY" DOES NOT MEAN "AT PRESENT" OR "NOW." "IS ARRIVING PRESENTLY" MEANS "IS ARRIVING SOON" OR "SHORTLY," NOT "IS ARRIVING NOW." THE USAGE OF BOTH "PRESENTLY" AND "TIMELY" IS CHANGING; IT PROBABLY IS BEST TO AVOID USING THEM.

| | |
|---|---|
| on-time (at the proper time) | The control-logic circuits effect the *timely* transfer of data. |
| | then / later / on-time |
| now | Three half-ton trucks have been bought and are *presently* in use. |
| | now / at the same time / only |

| | |
|---|---|
| first (earliest) | We got our *initial* parameters from the graphic analysis. |
| | first / only / premier |
| before | It is best to check the handler *previous to* live runs. |
| | after / before / at the time of |
| Later (after that) | *Subsequently* we used absorption cells with longer path lengths. |
| | soon / later / thereafter |
| on time (the completion of your project *on time*.) | This schedule ensures the *timely* completion of your project. |
| | on time / early / final |
| now | Discard commercial radios *currently* in use. |
| | now / presently / then |
| then | The other approach clips the speech signal, *thereafter* removes the noise with a gating circuit. |
| | finally / then / at some future date |
| later | The converters can be installed *at some future date*. |
| | first / later / earlier |
| now | We are *presently* studying a newly patented device. |
| | about to / now / on the present occasion · |
| soon | We expect *in the near future* to develop lasing with the rotating prism. |
| | soon / then / now |
| times | There may be *occasions* when radiation in all directions is desirable |
| | later / times / places |
| at first | Note that *initially* C rises with the increasing voltage. |
| | then / at first / now |

| first | Set down the conditions for growth *as a preliminary.* |
| | then / first / at present |
| after | *Subsequent to* that project, our company manufactured the following adaptors: . . . |
| | after / during / posterior to |

## 8-4 Review

Continue reviewing each frame, paying attention to the direct impact of the simpler term:

| *REPLACE OVERWEIGHT EXPRESSIONS WITH "AND," "OF," "FOR," OR "IF"* | |
| If | *In the event* they cannot furnish transportation, we will. |
| and | Our company also developed and manufactured Sidebender *as well as* its checkout system. |
| for | We analyzed this problem graphically *to provide* indications of system performance and for system parameters. |
| . . . for final calculations | This information goes to the processor *where* final calculations *are accomplished.* |
| *If* (when) a receiver *connects* (is connected) to | In the case of a receiver connecting to a trunk line, the receiver signals that addresses should be sent. |
| for | *To achieve* maximum gain, use the lowest value of $t_{min}$. |
| . . . the locations *of* interruptions. | The signals show the locations *at which* interruptions *occur.* |
| and | He also tabulated the test results for both experienced listeners *as well as* for the entire jury. |
| For (With) | *In the case of* systems such as GaSb:InAs, you will need finer resolution. |

| | |
|---|---|
| for | Formant location alone gives enough information *to permit* phoneme recognition. |
| and | We will increase the rate of energy delivery with more efficient discharge circuits *together with* smaller storage capacitors. |

## REPLACE WEIGHTY EXPRESSIONS WITH "SO," "AS," "ON," OR "IN"

| | |
|---|---|
| so | This application affects the porous material *in such a manner* that leakage does not occur. |
| as | The combinations turned up *in the fashion* shown in Figure 2. |
| in | The newer design aids *toward* lowering the cost. |
| So | *In order* that the compatibility of the system could be maintained, we rejected that device. |
| on | A track is a line *around* the circumference of the drum. |

## REPLACE OVERWEIGHT EXPRESSIONS WITH "TO," "BY," OR "WITH"

| | |
|---|---|
| with (by) | This can be done *by using* a vertical half-wave dipole. |
| to (or: . . . *if* operating techniques *change?*) | How will operators react *in the event of* changes in operating techniques? |
| by | The antenna is driven *through* the motor. |
| by (*with* a voice-excited vocoder.) | We can solve this problem *through* using a voice-excited vocoder. |

## REPLACE OVERWEIGHT QUANTITY EXPRESSIONS WITH ONE SUGGESTED

| | |
|---|---|
| also (We have also) | *In addition* we have surveyed all sites. |
| | since then / also / lately |
| *about* the same size and weight. | The two swivels are *in* the same size and weight *range*. |
| | larger / about / often |

| | |
|---|---|
| highest | At the *maximum* rate this is how we derived a batch of data: . . .<br><br>largest / highest / culminating |
| more than | This circuit limits the gain of amplifiers whose outputs change *in excess of* 10 decibels.<br><br>more than / about / most |
| Most (Much) | They used a *major portion* of the data in deriving these results.<br><br>some / most / all |
| at least | Delivery is a *minimum of* eighteen months away.<br><br>about / over / at least |
| many kinds | This site has a *large variety* of transportable equipment.<br><br>some kinds / many kinds / most kinds |
| also (Our system also) | *In addition* our system conforms to the standards for radio-propagation systems. |
| longest | This table specifies the *maximum* times between tests.<br><br>greatest / highest / longest |
| much | A *great deal of* redundancy remains.<br><br>some / much / all |
| often enough | Calibrate each station *with sufficient frequency* to maintain the evaluation ratio.<br><br>often enough / more / soon |
| better (give better results and are . . .) | Some deformations are *more optimum* and easier to handle.<br><br>higher / better / longer |
| earlier | *Previous* research led to the following: . . .<br><br>later / earlier / first |
| before | Fractions are rounded off *prior to* being read onto magnetic tape.<br><br>after / earlier than / before |

| | |
|---|---|
| now (already) | They are *presently* using this cathode in proto-type batteries. |
| | soon / then / now |
| first (early, earliest) | Our *initial* emphasis was on a low-cost, high-efficiency converter. |
| | latest / new / first |
| at the same time | Our department can design both verniers *concurrently*. |
| | at the same time / soon / now |
| before | *Prior to* depositing the metal layer heat the silicon in a partial pressure of hydrogen. |
| | when / before / earlier than |
| now | This is the lamp socket supplied *at present*. |
| | then / now / immediately |
| necessary | When *requirements warrant*, you can increase the concentration. |
| | necessary / you desire |

# LEAN VERBS

As we have already noted, verbs are action words. Their dynamism multiplies the impact of unnecessary meanings, with the result that heavyweight verbs overwhelm comprehension.

### 9-1 "Use" instead of "Utilize" and "Employ"

"Utilize" and "employ" often appear as weighty substitutes for "use." Yet these three words are not equivalent. They all carry the sense of availing of something. But "utilize" suggests also an ingenuity in putting to profitable use, and "employ" suggests also the putting to use of something that has been idle. "Use," however, conveys none of these additional meanings. For this reason, "employs" is ponderous in:

**The present accounting load** *employs* **(uses) only half the computer capacity.**

After replacing verbs in the following sentences with "use," check left to be sure you have the proper form. Then review the frame, noting the difference between the two verbs. The overweight verbs in the problem sentences are in italics.

*REPLACE OVERWEIGHT VERBS WITH FORMS OF "USE"*

| | |
|---|---|
| used | They *utilized* his findings in the manned-spacecraft program. |
| using | We are now *employing* more efficient discharge circuits. |

| | |
|---|---|
| use | They *utilize* aircraft to transport men between sites during the surveys. |

## 9-2 "Make" instead of "Fabricate" and "Construct"

"Make" can replace many weighty verbs. When it does, politicians can again get around to "making decisions" instead of "exercising options." The following sentences have other ponderous substitutes for "make," such as "implement," "incorporate," and "construct."

### REPLACE OVERWEIGHT VERBS WITH FORMS OF "MAKE"

| | |
|---|---|
| made | They *implemented* this system of a conventional PCM encoder and decoder and two pseudorandom noise generators. |
| make | You have to *accomplish* the test next month. |
| Make | *Initiate* a telephone call as follows: "first . . . ; then . . . ; next . . ." |
| made | Give the status of all changes being *incorporated* in the new models. |
| made | We *fabricated* a second lasing diode last month. |

## 9-3 "Use" and "Make" Combined

### REPLACE OVERWEIGHT VERBS WITH FORMS OF "USE" OR OF "MAKE"

| | |
|---|---|
| uses | The 4,000 Megahertz (or Megacycles) system *utilizes* power outputs of 1 watt, 10 watts, and 1 kilowatt. |
| made | We *constructed* this unit before the alloy was available. |
| made of (use) | Our engineers recommend that the digital encoding system be *implemented of* DVS logic-limiting circuits. |
| made | Changes must be *incorporated* in three stages. |

| | |
|---|---|
| made | He based this design on a study he *performed* last year. |
| use | Our system will *employ* only 120 communications channels. |
| makes | Our Rocky Mountain plant *produces* this specialized electronic equipment. |
| made | After that project, we *manufactured* the evaporators. |
| being made | This compressor is now *under construction.* . . . is now being |
| use | You can also *employ* separate gating circuits. |
| Make | *Accomplish* the change by replacing the I-F strips. |

COMMENT: "ACCOMPLISH" MEANS "MAKE," "DO," OR "CARRY OUT," WHICH MEANS THAT THE FOLLOWING SENTENCE IS NONSENSE:

Flexible wiring can *accomplish* (make, do, carry out) the desired design.

THE WRITER DEPENDED UNTHINKINGLY ON A WORD HE WASN'T IN CONTROL OF. WHAT HE MEANT WAS PROBABLY THAT:

*With* flexible wiring the desired design can be *carried out.*

## 9-4  "Check" instead of "Ascertain" and "Verify"; "Causes" instead of "Is Responsible For"

The following problem sentences rely on two types of unnecessarily ponderous verbs. You can replace one with forms of "check" or "be sure" and the other with forms of "cause."

*REPLACE VERBS WITH "CHECK" OR "CAUSE"*

| | |
|---|---|
| Check (Learn if) | *Ascertain* that they have finished the adjustment and installation phase. |
| as caused by | The change can be explained *in terms of* diffuse surface reflection. . . . explained as ———— by. . . . |
| causes | The heat *accomplishes* the breakup. |

| | |
|---|---|
| checked (out) (tested) | We *evaluated* the processor with a TPS-1D radar set. |
| Check | *Inspect* the door catch for sticking. |
| causes | In films less than 100 angstroms thick, agglomeration *is responsible for* the increase. |
| cause | Does lattice mismatch *give rise to* interfacial dislocations? |
| Check (Be sure) | *Verify* that the adjustment is correct. |
| Check (Be sure) | *Ascertain* that each assembly is warming up. |
| caused all absorption to occur in. . . . | This increase *resulted in* all the absorption occurring in the field. (Use "to occur.") |
| caused by | Other writers attributed this to dissociation of the films *due to* the vapor pressure. |
| Check (Be sure) | *Confirm* that the START push button lights. |
| caused | This arcing *resulted in* fractures. |
| caused | Surface scattering *was responsible* for the difference from bulk resistance. |
| Check (Be sure) | *Ensure* that all indicators are blinking green. |
| as caused by | The increase can be explained *in terms of* diffuse surface reflection. |
| | . . . explained as _____ by diffuse. . . . |

COMMENT: OVERLOADED WORDS, IN ADDITION TO BEARING SUPERFLUOUS INFORMATION, OFTEN DRAG OTHER BAGGAGE IN THEIR TRAIN. IN THE FOLLOWING SENTENCE "VERIFY" NECESSITATES THE INCLUSION OF "ARE PRODUCED":

*To verify* that adverse effects *are not produced,* we will measure the resistance and mobility before and after processing.

"CHECK" ELIMINATES THE REFERENCE TO PRODUCTION:

*To check* for adverse effects we will measure the. . . .

## 9-5 "Has" instead of "Is Equipped With" and "Exhibit"

*REPLACE HEAVYWEIGHT VERBS WITH FORMS OF "HAS"*

| | |
|---|---|
| have (show) | The diodes should *exhibit* a high plate-to-cathode resistance. |

| have | Each room will *be equipped with* two humidifiers. |
|---|---|
| have (show) | Films of 100 percent zinc sulfide *exhibit* a cubic structure. |
| had | Our men have *encountered* much difficulty getting adequate transportation. |
| has | Each position *is provided with* a knob for controlling light intensity. |
| has | Each site *is equipped with* the same test equipment. |

COMMENT: CAESAR'S "I CAME, I SAW, I CONQUERED" FOGGED IN WITH PRETENTIOUS PONDEROSITY COMES OUT LIKE THIS:

I appeared; I beheld: I vanquished.

AND STUFFED WITH DEADWOOD:

I appeared on the scene of encounter; I beheld the tactical situation: I vanquished the opposition.

THE ROMAN SAID IT MORE SIMPLY AND FORCEFULLY.

## 9-6 "Give" instead of "Provide" and "Present"

The following sentences rely on weighty replacements for "give," words like "provides" in:

**"One reading** *provides* **(gives) enough information."**

### REPLACE LOADED VERBS WITH FORMS OF "GIVE"

| give | You must establish a need-to-know before we can *promulgate* this information to you. |
|---|---|
| gives (has) | Volume 3 *presents* the troubleshooting information. |
| give | The formant locations alone *provide* enough information for phoneme recognition. |
| give (or: . . . spend . . . on) | The employees listed below will *contribute* all their time to this project. |
| give | Before we can *furnish* you more specific information, you have to satisfy security requirements. |

| | |
|---|---|
| gives | The transparent, pivoted door *permits* access to the working parts. |
| give | We *present* their comments below. |

## 9-7 "Show" and "Send" instead of "Illustrate" and "Disseminate"

"Illustrate" says much more than "show," and "disseminate" says more than "send." Use the simpler verbs where they are adequate.

*REPLACE VERBS WITH "SHOW" OR "SEND"*

| | |
|---|---|
| showed (explained) | Last month's report *demonstrated* the practicability of linking the scanners. |
| shows | This chart *illustrates* where the problem is. |
| sends | The timer *transmits* its signals through the clock system. |
| shows | Our performance on earlier contracts *demonstrates* that we are qualified to carry out these surveys. |
| show (read) | The meter should *indicate* −20 dbm. |
| send | These circuits *supply* a signal to the switching circuits in the synchronizer. |
| show | These plots *indicate* the improvement you can expect. |
| shows | Figure 5 *illustrates* the major steps. |
| show (will have lost no power) | The received signal will *exhibit* no loss of power. |
| sent (Delays are immediately reported. . . .) | Information about delays is *disseminated* immediately to all departments. |

COMMENT: DO NOT JUST AUTOMATICALLY SUBSTITUTE LIGHTWEIGHT WORDS FOR WEIGHTIER ONES, OR SOMETIMES YOU WILL CHANGE THE INTENDED MESSAGE. IF THE WEIGHTIER WORD FITS, USE IT. THE TECHNICIAN WHO WROTE THE FOLLOWING SENTENCE MIGHT HAVE MEANT NO MORE THAN THAT SIGNALS ARE SENT:

Fault signals are *directed* (sent) to the operator's console.

BUT IF HE ALSO MEANT THAT THE SIGNAL IS GUIDED TO THE CONSOLE, THEN "SENT" WOULD BE LESS PRECISE; "DIRECTED" WOULD BE CORRECT.

## 9-8  "Need" and "Call For" instead of "Require"

"Require" carries a strong sense of constraint from its use in mathematics and law. Avoid it where you can use simpler verbs.

### REPLACE "REQUIRES" WITH "NEEDS" OR "CALLS FOR"

| | |
|---|---|
| needs (calls for) | One-bit logic *requires* less power. |
| needed | The 70 Megahertz (or Megacycles) intermediate amplifier gives the gain and selectivity *required* to load the channel. |
| needed | This will reduce the percentage of the bit rate *required* for hybrid excitation. |
| needed (called for) | Adjustments of the radius arms are not *required*. |
| needed | This table lists the special tools, test jigs, and fixtures *required* to service the gyro. |

COMMENT: READABILITY STUDIES SHOW THAT PONDEROUS VOCABULARIES INTERFERE WITH UNDERSTANDING. SIMPLE WORDS GET MESSAGES ACROSS MORE EFFICIENTLY.

## 9-9  "Begin" and "End" instead of "Initiate" and "Terminate"

The verbs in the following sentences have to do with starting and ending.

### REPLACE VERBS WITH "BEGIN" OR "END," "START" OR "FINISH"

| | |
|---|---|
| end (stop, finish) | This will *terminate* the tests. |
| begin (start) | We can *initiate* site surveys immediately. |
| began (started on) | Our research department then *embarked on* an independent program. |
| end (finish) | *Terminate* a telephone call as follows: . . . |
| begin (start) | Work will *commence* immediately on award of contract. |
| end (finish) | We will *conclude* the optical and structural studies during the next report period. |

| | |
|---|---|
| start (. . . start the motor.) | Next, have the operator *initiate* the operation of the motor. (If you can, remove "operation.") |

## 9-10 "Is" instead of Ponderous Verbs

We have twice dealt with "be" verbs, such as "is," "are," "was," and "were." First, they were an element in passive voice forms, as in "*is* settled." Later they were weak verbs which hid more descriptive verbs, as in "is dependent," which became "depends." We now turn to sentences which are saddled with ponderous verbs, but which need nothing more than a "be" verb. The following sentence is an example. It needs a verb that does little more than connect the expressions on either side of it.

**Figure 5** *shows* **(is) a photograph of the operator's cab.**

"Is" is adequate for that job: it acts as little more than an identity sign.

### *REPLACE VERBS WITH FORMS OF "BE"*

| | |
|---|---|
| be | The cost may *prove* prohibitive. |
| was (is) | He chose a cathode ray tube because it *represented* the only inexpensive, high-quality display. |
| are (stand for) | The points on the graph *represent* the new data. |
| are | These cards *form* the program deck. |
| is (is square.) | The indicator *consists of* a square area. ("Area" becomes superfluous) |
| is | The primary drawback *lies in* that sometimes corrosion losses are prohibitive. |
| is | The display equipment *consists of* an integrally housed unit containing the video and processing circuits. |

You will have to rewrite the following sentences slightly:

| | |
|---|---|
| is compatible | The commercial equipment now in use *offers compatibility* with the government equipment. (Use "compatible.") |

| | |
|---|---|
| is 2 inches deep | The card reader *has* a 2-inch depth. (Use "deep.") |
| was | Our assembly *proved to be* the faster. (Keep in past tense.) |
| is not clear. | The writing *lacks* clarity. (Use "not clear.") |
| is (or: . . . is more complex because) | The serial system *results in* a more complex system because it uses extra buffers. |
| is (will be) | The Indo-European communications system *envisions* a long-distance telephone and teletype system. |
| is easy to interpret | The square pattern of the B-scan *lends itself to* easy interpretation. (Use "to interpret.") |

COMMENT: EVEN SHAKESPEARE PREFERRED "BE" TO THE PHILOSOPHICALLY WEIGHTY "EXISTS." "TO BE OR NOT TO BE," HE WROTE; NOT "TO EXIST OR NOT TO EXIST. . . ." OR EVEN "TO EXIST OR THE CONTRARY. . . ." "EXIST" IS ALSO TOO HEAVY IN THE FOLLOWING WARNING:

Dangerous voltages *exist* in this cabinet.

THIS COULD BE:

Voltages in this cabinet *are* dangerous.

OR JUST:

Dangerous voltages.


## 9-11 "Change," "Bought," or "Set Up"

*REPLACE VERBS WITH "CHANGE," "BOUGHT," OR "SET UP"*

| | |
|---|---|
| changes | During evaporation, the composition of the vapor *varies* continually. |
| bought | Three trucks have been *purchased*. |
| set up | We have *established* three indoctrination centers. |
| changed | The output *varied* more than 50 decibels. |
| set up | At that time we will *establish* the organization to carry out this tunneling. |
| bought | We *purchased* the same type of crystal in raw form. |

| set up | We have already *established* extensive on-the-job training programs for local employees. |
| --- | --- |

## 9-12   Other Light Verbs

The following sentences have a variety of other overweight verbs. Possible replacements are given in each frame. Be sure to keep the original meaning.

### *CIRCLE THE SIMPLER REPLACEMENT*

| increase | The trailers greatly *enhance* mobility and flexibility. |
| --- | --- |
| | brighten / increase / decrease |
| Turn | *Rotate* the handcrank fully clockwise. |
| | Turn / Shift / Gyrate |
| Do (Carry out, Run, Make) | *Perform* this test first. |
| | Shift / Do / Accomplish |
| increases | Raising the collector voltage *enhances* current gain. |
| | enlightens / increases / multiplies |
| Turn | *Rotate* the potentiometer counterclockwise. |
| | Adjust / Align / Turn |
| carry out (do, make) | With the equipment on this list, you can *accomplish* all these tests. |
| | express / carry out / foul up |
| knows | Everyone *is aware* of this problem. |
| | knows / apprehends / comprehends |
| Do (Carry out, Make) | *Perform* the following analyses: . . . |
| | Operate / Do / Accomplish |
| know | We *are aware* of no fundamental limitation on the pulse rate. |
| | know / are cognizant / apprehend |

| | |
|---|---|
| does (carries out) | The alternate core memory *performs* this operation in half the time. |
| | does / operates / accomplishes |
| do (finish) | You have to *achieve* most of the cost analysis in the time between the two phases. |
| | perform / accomplish / do |
| listed (named) | The reports we will turn in are *stipulated* in the contract. |
| | listed / contained / expressed |
| keep | This arrangement will *maintain* the floor load below the limit of 150 pounds per square foot. |
| | keep / foster / substantiate |
| does | Our newer calculator *performs* all three jobs at the same time. |
| | does / accomplishes / finalizes |
| keep | The air conditioners will *maintain* the temperature below 80°F. |
| | keep / increase / stabilize |
| judged (thought) | As *deemed* necessary, report the results to your department head. |
| | conceived / judged / fancied |
| believe (expect) | We *anticipate* that this change will not shift the breakpoint. |
| | surmise / believe / opine |
| gained | Our company *acquired* much experience in concentric loading. |
| | procured / secured / gained |
| reduces (cuts) | The new vocoder *minimizes* the differences in outputs. |
| | moderates / converts / reduces |
| answer | The next chapter explains how to *respond to* a call. |
| | reciprocate / answer / react |

| | |
|---|---|
| lowers (cuts) | A simple design also *minimizes* costs. |
| | moderates / diminishes / lowers |
| going | Do not disconnect the test leads when *proceeding* from one step to the next. |
| | going / progressing / operating |

COMMENT: "CONFIGURE" AND "CONFIGURATION" ARE OFTEN USED PRETENTIOUSLY. THEY CAN USUALLY BE REPLACED BY SIMPLER WORDS LIKE "ARRANGE," "LAYOUT," "DISPOSE," AND "PATTERN": "FIGURE 4 SHOWS THE FIRST *CONFIGURATION* (ARRANGEMENT, LAYOUT)." OFTEN, HOWEVER, THESE WEIGHTY WORDS ARE WHOLLY UNNECESSARY. THE PERSON WHO WROTE:

How will changes in equipment configuration affect the communications system?

INTENDED TO SAY JUST:

How will changes in equipment affect the . . . system?

| | |
|---|---|
| stands for (is from) | The solid curve *represents* measurements on bulk material. |
| | exhibits / delineates / stands for |
| listed (named) | In addition to those *stipulated* in the specifications, we will also include a report for Station XII. |
| | listed / enumerated / designated |
| want to study | We *are desirous of studying* the effects of radiation. |
| | want to study / need to study / have to study |
| put in (use, add) | You should *introduce* another Y unit. |
| | incorporate / inaugurate / put in |
| got | We *obtained* the first curves from the graphic analysis. |
| | acquired / got / procured |
| decided (fixed, set) | We have not yet *resolved* on our course. |
| | decided / determined / concluded |

COMMENT: THE WRITER OF THE FOLLOWING SENTENCE OVERBURDENED HIMSELF AND AS A RESULT DIDN'T NOTICE HE WAS NOT SAYING WHAT HE WANTED TO. WRITING ABOUT MEASUREMENTS MADE *ON* ANNEALED FILMS, HE WROTE:

Most of the measurements *employed* annealed films.

**HAD HE LESS PONDEROUSLY WRITTEN:**

Most of the measurements *used* annealed films.

**HE WOULD HAVE SEEN HOW THIS CONFLICTED WITH HIS INTENDED MESSAGE ABOUT THE MEASUREMENTS BEING MADE ON ANNEALED FILMS. THE OVERWEIGHT VERB MADE IT DIFFICULT FOR HIM TO SEE HIS ERROR.**

## 9-13  Review

The following frames will reinforce what you have been learning in this chapter. Continue reviewing each frame before leaving it.

### REPLACE VERBS WITH "USE," "MAKE," OR "CHECK"

| | |
|---|---|
| made | They used that data in designing the tracker now being *constructed*. |
| use | These antennas *utilize* dual diversity. |
| made (put together) | We *fabricated* two new test setups. |
| use | The other eight channels *employ* one-bit modulators. |
| Check | *Inspect* the flanges for looseness. |
| use | Our engineers tested card readers that *utilize* photoconductor cells and fiber optics. |
| Check | *Verify* that the facsimile recorder has been wired properly. |

### REPLACE VERBS WITH "GIVE," "NEED," "END," OR "BEGIN" ("START")

| | |
|---|---|
| needs | In normal operation this generator *requires* no adjustment. |
| begin (start) (begin to redesign) | We will *initiate* redesign of the sprinkler. |
| gives (brings) | Their highest value *provides* some benefits. |
| starts (begins) | This switch *initiates* the process. |
| needs (calls for) | Alternate II *requires* no additional scanning. |

| | |
|---|---|
| begin (start) | The study will *commence* even before the contract is awarded. |
| ended | The planning *terminated* too soon. |
| gives (has) | The servicing handbook also *provides* operating instructions. |
| needed | The tables on the facing page give other information *required* to align the receiver. |
| gives (lists, shows) | Figure 1 *presents* the sediment distribution. |

## REPLACE VERBS WITH "BE" OR "HAS"

| | |
|---|---|
| has | The automatic cutout *is provided with* a manual override. |
| is | The most important feature of making this transistor *lies* in preparing the semiconductor for mating to the base. |
| have (need, take longer to deliver.) | Such supplies *require* longer delivery times. |
| have (show) | These circuits *exhibit* a high ratio of capacitive-to-inductive reactance. |
| is (has) | Figure 3 *shows* a wiring diagram of the circuit. |
| have | The batteries now *provide* taps for 20 milliamperes only. |

## REPLACE VERBS WITH "SHOW," "THINK," "BUY," OR "SEND"

| | |
|---|---|
| show | These signals *indicate* the locations of surges. |
| thought (judged, believed) | Our experts *deemed* transportation by air necessary. |
| bought | They then *purchased* the steel tanks from a local dealer. |
| showed | These studies *demonstrated* the practicability of this feed horn. |
| sent (given) | This bulletin is *disseminated* to all supervisors. |

| think (expect, believe) | We *anticipate* that other lines will connect through this station. |
| --- | --- |

COMMENT: POSSIBLY, WRITERS COME TO RELY ON OVERLOADED AND POMPOUS WORDS FROM FOLLOWING A COROLLARY TO THE DICTUM THAT "CLOTHES MAKE THE MAN," SUPPOSING THAT "WORDS MAKE THE MESSAGE." NOTHING COULD BE FURTHER FROM THE TRUTH. JUST AS THE MAN ALONE MAKES THE MAN, SO THE MESSAGE ALONE MAKES THE MESSAGE. RATHER THAN "MAKING THE MESSAGE," OVERLOADED WORDS DETRACT FROM IT.

# AUXILIARY VERBS

Auxiliary verbs are words like "can," "help," and "must." They work with or help another verb, as in "*can* decide," "*helps* decide," and "*must* decide." Here the auxiliaries work with the main verb, "decide." They express fine shades of meaning and emphasis and help avoid cumbersome expressions.

## 10-1  "Can" Verbs from "-ble" Words

"Can" is discreetly vague and impersonal and can replace many overweight expressions. The following sentence, for example, relies on a combination of a "be" verb with a fairly long word that ends in "-ble":

**These spectrophotometers** *are repairable* **in the field.**

This combination can be replaced with "can" and a verb made from the "-ble" word ("repairable"):

**These spectrophotometers** *can be repaired* **in the field.**

This replaces the "be" verb ("are") with the stronger, more descriptive verb "can be repaired." The expressions on the left below can be revised similarly:

"is transportable" becomes "can be transported."
"are avoidable" becomes "can be avoided."
"is expansible" becomes "can be expanded."

Recast the following sentences similarly. Keep the original subject; replace the "be" verb with "can" and a new verb made from the "-ble" word.

## REWRITE WITH "CAN" AND A NEW VERB

| | |
|---|---|
| can be transported | The larger van *is transportable in* C-123s.<br>The larger van can be _____ |
| can be expanded | Their switching network *is expandable* without interrupting service.<br>Their . . . network can be |
| can be adjusted (to transmit) | The 40-kilowatt power amplifier is adjustable for transmission at lower power. |
| can be turned | Fixed-station antennas are turnable by a simple mechanical adjustment. |
| can be repeated | This concentration is repeatable to within 5 percent of the reading over the entire range. |

**COMMENT: NOTE THAT MANY OF THE PRECEDING REVISIONS RESULT IN PASSIVE-VOICE VERBS:**

Their switching network *can be expanded.*

**WHERE FITTING IN YOUR OWN WRITING, CHANGE THESE TO ACTIVE VOICE:**

They *can expand* their switching network.

### 10-2  "Can" Verbs from Non "-ble" Words

The new verbs for the following sentences do not come from the "-ble" words. In the following, "to respond" is the potential verb:

**The project manager** *is able to respond* **(can respond) immediately to reports of trouble.**

In the following, "to be done" is the potential verb:

**This** *is not able to be done.*

which becomes:

**This** *cannot* **be done.**

In a similar way, the "-ble" expressions on the left change to "can" expressions like those on the right.

"is possible to run" becomes "can run."

"has the ability to reverse" becomes "can reverse."
"are amenable to manufacture" becomes "can be manufactured."
"is capable of searching" becomes "can search."
"Control of X is available" becomes "X can be controlled."

## REWRITE WITH "CAN"

| | |
|---|---|
| can be manufactured from | They *are amenable* to *manufacture* from solid-state silicon. |
| | They can be |
| can be increased. | *It is possible to increase* the response at 15 kilocycles. |
| | The response at 15 kilocycles can be |
| can be fed. | It is possible to feed either two or three branches. |
| | Either two or three branches can be |
| cannot be printed on. . . . | Printed-wire crossovers are impossible to print on a plane surface. |
| | . . . crossovers cannot be |
| can also be controlled. | Also available are control of pitch inflection and voice quality. |
| | Pitch . . . and voice . . . can also be |
| can present | The common display circuits *have the ability to present* the information listed below. |
| can carry | This model is capable of carrying three men for moon exploration. |
| can search | The radar is capable of searching a sector of approximately 900 meters at a range rate of 7 seconds per sector. |

## 10-3  "Help" instead of "Was Instrumental In"

Replace weighty expressions in the following frames with the auxiliary verb "help" and a new verb; for example:

**He** *was instrumental in creating* **(helped create)** the only . . .

## *REWRITE WITH "HELP"*

| | |
|---|---|
| helps lower | A simple process *lends itself to lowering* the production cost. |
| | A simple process helps |
| helped develop (improve) | He *worked on the development of* improved black-and-white television receivers. |
| | He helped |
| helps keep | The diversion of the coolant aids in keeping the R-F cavities tuned. |
| might help reduce the weight. | Other devices might provide weight *reduction*. |
| | Other devices might _____ the weight. |
| will help develop the | Our human-factors engineers will participate in the development of the man-machine combinations. |

## 10-4 "Must" and "Have To" Instead of "Is Necessary," "Is Essential"

The following problem sentences contain weighty and long expressions of obligation, such as "is necessary," "is essential," and "is the responsibility of." The obligation can be conveyed more directly by "must" or "have to" and a new verb. For example;

**Control** of the beam voltage *is essential*.

can become:

**The beam voltage** *must be controlled.*

## *REWRITE WITH "MUST" OR "HAS TO"*

| | |
|---|---|
| do not have to be created (need not be created.) | These programs are so designed that the *creation* of new tests *is unnecessary*. |
| | . . . that new tests do not have to be |
| We must select | We are required to select a program that will reduce processing time. |
| | We must |

| | |
|---|---|
| Excess solder must be removed. | *Removal of* excess solder is *mandatory*. |
| The user must follow (must see that) . . . | The user is responsible for seeing that these instructions are followed. |
| do not have to be created (or: . . . need not be created.) | The tapes can be coordinated so that the creation of intermediate tapes is not necessary.<br><br>. . . so that intermediate tapes do not |

The following sentences express obligation through an anticipatory subject, "it." "It" becomes superfluous, as in:

*It is necessary to discover, reliable collection and classification techniques.*

which becomes:

**Reliable collection and classification techniques** *must be discovered.*

## REWRITE WITH "MUST" OR "HAS TO"

| | |
|---|---|
| must be found. | *It is necessary to find* the correct ratio.<br><br>The correct ratio must |
| The data must be arranged<br><br>(The data must be in an arrangement. . . .) | It is essential that the data be in an arrangement compatible with the address words in the drum.<br><br>The data must |
| One must (be able to) produce. . . . | It is imperative that one be able to produce predictable, repeatable electric properties.<br><br>One |
| . . . of the magnetic field has to be adjusted. | To focus the beam, it is only necessary to adjust the strength of the magnetic field.<br><br>To focus the beam, only the strength of the |

**COMMENT: YOU CAN SEE GOOD REASONS FOR OBJECTING TO POMPOUS WRITING BY TRYING TO GET AT THE MEANING OF THE FOLLOWING SENTENCE:**

These improvements *are conducive to* least cost in production.

**THIS MIGHT MEAN:**

These improvements *will help achieve* the *least cost* in production.

**WHICH MIGHT MEAN:**

These improvements will help achieve the *lowest possible* production *cost.*

**OR IT MIGHT MEAN:**

These improvements *will* (*help*) *lower* the cost of production.

**OR EVEN:**

These improvements *will lower* the cost.

**WHICH IS PROBABLY WHAT THE WRITER SHOULD HAVE WRITTEN IN THE FIRST PLACE, RATHER THAN GETTING HUNG UP ON THE HEAVYWEIGHT "CONDUCIVE," THE JARGON "LEAST COST," AND THE PROBABLY SUPERFLUOUS "IN PRODUCTION."**

## 10-5   Unnecessary Auxiliary Verbs

It often turns out that the auxiliary verb is not needed. Consider the sentence:

**This synthesizer** *is capable of generating* **words of up to four phonemes.**

which becomes:

**This synthesizer** *can generate* **words of.** . . .

"Can generate" hints that human intervention is needed for the generating to take place. But this need can be taken for granted. We can state an actuality:

**This synthesizer** *generates* **words of.** . . .

This revision resembles the development of dynamic verbs.

### *REWRITE WITHOUT AUXILIARY VERBS*

| | |
|---|---|
| still maintains stable flight. | At its absolute ceiling, the missile still *is able to* (*can*) *maintain* stable flight.<br><br>. . . the missile still |
| reduces | The high-speed transfer rate *permits reduction of* (*can reduce*) the amount of equipment needed at each site. |
| raises | The new blend aids in raising (helps raise) the yield. |
| measures | The ohmeter permits measurement of resistance. |

COMMENT: ADVERTISING WRITERS CREATE IMMEDIACY BY STRESSING ACTUALITIES RATHER THAN POSSIBILITIES. NOT:

This automobile *can speed* up to 140 miles an hour.

BUT:

This automobile *speeds* up to 140 miles an hour.

| | |
|---|---|
| retain | The flat roof and the parapets allow the retention of rainwater. |
| recognizes | This device is capable of recognizing (can recognize) many other fonts. |
| selects | Selector switch S1 *allows selection of* A, B, or C. |

COMMENT: DON'T JUST INDISCRIMINATELY REMOVE AUXILIARY VERBS. IF MORE THAN ONE PERSON PARTICIPATED IN THE CREATION OF A NEW DEVICE, IT WOULD BE WRONG TO SHORTEN "HE *HELPED CREATE* . . ." TO "HE *CREATED*. . . ." SIMILARLY, IT WOULD BE WRONG TO CHANGE:

Factors other than engineering merit *help determine* the effectiveness of proposals.''

TO:

Factors other than engineering merit *determine* the effectiveness. . . .''

THE SECOND SENTENCE SAYS THAT ENGINEERING MERIT IS NOT A FACTOR IN DETERMINING PROPOSAL EFFECTIVENESS, WHICH IS NOT WHAT THE FIRST SENTENCE CLAIMS.

## 10-6 "Tells How To" instead of "Provides Information For."

Many weighty expressions phrased as though to give information are actually intended as instructions. The overweight jargon says something like:

**This section** *contains information on aligning and adjusting* **the assembly. (or ". . . gives the theory of alignment and. . . .")**

when what is meant is:

**This section** *explains how to align and adjust* **the assembly. (or: ". . . tells how to. . . .")**

In the following sentences, keep the original subject, and replace weighty expressions with "explains how," developing infinitives as needed.

## REWRITE WITH "EXPLAINS HOW" OR "HOW TO"

| | |
|---|---|
| explains (tells) how to maintain | This chapter *contains information on main-taining* the synchronizer.<br><br>This chapter explains how to |
| explains (tells) how both circuits operate. | This section *discusses the theory of operation of* both circuits.<br><br>This section explains how both |

## IN THE FOLLOWING SENTENCES CONTINUE INSERTING "EXPLAINS HOW (HOW TO)" OR "TELLS HOW (HOW TO)"

| | |
|---|---|
| explains (tells) how to operate | This booklet *contains instructions for oper-ating* the camera under normal conditions. |
| explain (tell) how to prestart and to apply power. | The paragraphs that follow provide instruc-tions for prestart and for applying power. |
| explains how to time (how computer operations are timed.) | This section sets forth the methods used for timing computer operations. |
| explains (tells) how the interfer-ometer operates. | The next section *presents the theory of opera-tion of* the interferometer.<br><br>. . . explains how the interferometer |
| explains | The remainder of this paper *illustrates* how this problem was solved. |
| explain how to operate (how the . . . computer operates.) | These chapters *contain information relative to the operation of* the central computer. |

## 10-7 "Try" instead of "Attempt," "Make an Effort"

You can often use the simple "try" in place of expressions like "give attention to" and "attempt." The pompous "Innovative techniques will be *introduced*" might become "We will *try* something new." New subjects are suggested in the following frames. Rewrite the sentences with the subject and "try." For example, the follow-ing sentence might be rewritten with "we":

*Efforts will be made* **to study the rill.**

giving:

**We** *will try* **to study the rill.**

## REWRITE WITH "TRY"

| | |
|---|---|
| tried to conform | *Attention has been given to conforming* to the 6,000-mile standard-transmission path. |
| | We have tried to |
| They will try to reduce the | *An attempt will be made to reduce* the types of analog circuits. |
| | They will try |
| we will try to operate these | If time permits, *attempts will be made to operate* these junctions in lasing modes. |
| | If time permits, we will |
| will try to reduce the | Nevertheless, *efforts will be made to reduce* the density. |
| | Nevertheless, they will |
| We have tried to use the | We have given attention to using the injectors already installed. |
| | We |

## 10-8 Review

## REWRITE WITH "CAN"

| | |
|---|---|
| can extract and display (extracts and displays . . .) | This circuit is capable of extracting and displaying all the target data. (Two verbs) |
| can be varied from (can vary) | The 40,000-watt output *is variable* from 12,000 to 40,000 watts. |
| . . . .that can carry the information. | These filters have the narrowest bandwidth *capable of carrying* the information. |
| | . . . have the narrowest bandwidth that |
| the fields can be aligned mechanically. | The solution of these problems allows mechanical alignment of the fields. |
| | With the solution of these problems the fields can |

| | |
|---|---|
| A simple flow chart can be outlined. | *It is possible to outline* a simple flow chart. |
| . . . a true real-time system can be developed. | The direct transmission of data permits development of a true real-time system. |
| | With the direct transmission of data a true |
| that cannot be repaired at the site. | Section V explains how to remove and re-ship diesels that *are not repairable at the site*. |
| . . . we can place three command consoles. . . . | The completion of the new stations permits us to place three command consoles on each communications loop. |
| | With the completion of . . . we |
| Because of this feature the processor can be operated at any clock rate. (can operate) | This feature allows operation of the processor at any clock rate. |
| | Because of this feature, the processor |
| Now we can state the . . . | Now it is possible to state the real problem. |
| | Now we can |

## REWRITE WITH "EXPLAIN," "MUST," OR "HAVE TO"

| | |
|---|---|
| explains how to adjust (Unless the section contains only data.) | This section *contains the data for adjusting* the infrared thermometer. |
| explains (tells) how to maintain | This section *provides maintenance information for* the processor. |
| must design | We *are required to* design twenty-five card readers. |
| This road must be developed | *Development* of this road *is essential.* |
| explain (tell) how to test and adjust | Paragraphs 2-40 through 2-50 *present the procedures for* testing and adjusting the relays. |
| Vacuum deposition must be used. | It is necessary to use vacuum deposition. |
| | Vacuum deposition |
| The processor must have | It is necessary that the processor have five master boards. |
| explain (tell) how to remove | These paragraphs provide information on removal of the chassis. |

| | |
|---|---|
| These trucks must be provided | Provision of these trucks is essential if the job is to be finished on time. |
| | These trucks must be |
| The user must follow | It is the responsibility of the user to follow these safety precautions. |
| | The user must |
| | (If this were legal assignment of responsibility, it would have to be left unchanged.) |

COMMENT: SINGLE INSTANCES OF OVERWEIGHT OR PRETENTIOUS WORDS ARE TROUBLESOME, BUT THE UNUSED MEANINGS MISLEAD ONLY SLIGHTLY. YET WHEN A NUMBER OF THEM APPEAR TOGETHER, AS THEY USUALLY DO, AMBIGUITY AND OBSCURITY INCREASE GEOMETRICALLY. THIS IS BECAUSE OF THE INCREASED POSSIBLE INTERCONNECTIONS OF MEANINGS. SOME OF THE SUPERFLUOUS MEANINGS WILL INTERCONNECT; OTHERS WILL JUST SEEM TO. HOSTS OF POSSIBLE INTERCONNECTIONS BECOME CONFUSED WITH THE INTENDED ONES. THE RESULT IS A MUSH OF UNCLEAR WRITING. AVOID IT BY STICKING TO SIMPLE FAMILIAR WORDS WHEREVER THEY FIT.

## REWRITE WITH "HELP" AND "TRY"

| | |
|---|---|
| helps lower (lowers) | The rock base *aids in lowering* the cost. |
| tried | We *attempted to develop* a new type of lasing diode. |
| | We |
| helped develop | He *was instrumental in developing* phosphor technology. |
| will help design | As a project engineer you will work on the design of an infrared communications system. |
| tried to reduce | Our engineer-scientists have pursued the possibility of reducing these three parameters to a single equivalent parameter. |
| tried to fabricate | We *attempted to fabricate* lasing diodes between copper heat sinks. |

## REWRITE WITHOUT AUXILIARY VERBS

| | |
|---|---|
| satisfies | A variable gas semiconductor *allows satisfaction of* (*can satisfy*) these requirements. |
| reverses | This system is superior because it *has the ability to reverse* (*can reverse*) more rapidly. |

| | |
|---|---|
| offers (combines) | Our company can offer a strong combination of long experience and special equipment. |
| efficiently uses | This transistor structure permits the efficient use of (can efficiently use) the hot-electron phenomena. |
| selects | This circuit provides for selecting (can select) the desired frequencies. |

# OTHER PONDEROUS WRITING

This chapter completes our work with overloaded words. It then goes on to related factors that impede understanding, such as the use of many words where one would do and the use of general words when specific ones are available. The writers of many of these heavyweight sentences wrote this way because they were following the *sometimes* useful advice not to repeat words too frequently. To avoid repetitions, they sought out and used unusual, complex, and vague words; and sometimes they used simple words like pronouns without making clear what they refer to. These writers should have learned that clarity frequently demands repetition of words.

## 11-1  Ponderous Nouns

Many writers rely on overweight nouns, for example, using "philosophy," in "philosophy of system design," when it would be more precise to say "principles of system design." Here are a few nouns with their simpler replacements:

"personnel" and "associates" can be replaced by "employees," or "engineers"
"individuals" and "parties" can be replaced by "people" or "persons"
"variation" and "conversion" can be replaced by "change" or "difference"
"parameter" can be replaced by "limit," "value," or "characteristic"

Use the words in the left column when they can carry the desired meaning, that is, where the context takes advantage of all their meanings. Avoid these words when simpler, more direct words could do the job.

In the following sentences nouns are in parentheses. Circle the simpler noun.

In reviewing each frame, note the direct impact of the simpler word as compared with the other words.

## CIRCLE THE SIMPLER, MORE PRECISE WORD

| | |
|---|---|
| jobs | This file does all three (functions, jobs). |
| a study | Their report describes (an investigation, a study) of pollution they recently completed. |
| principles | Explain the (philosophy, principles) your company follows in designing systems. |
| change | The (change, conversion) from half-wave to full-wave rectification got rid of the 60-cycle ripple. |
| study | Further (study, examination) of the data brought out the cause of the ambiguity. |
| factors | Two (phenomena, factors) increased the strain. |
| types | We will supply three (types, categories) of reports. |
| study | We already have the sediment under (consideration, study). |
| plan | This is our basic (plan, concept) for increasing reliability. |
| employees | We have already set up similar programs for other local (personnel, employees, associates). |
| way | The original stop roller slowed the envelopes in a (fashion, way, mode) that occasionally burst their leading edge. |
| men | The (men, personnel, individuals) listed below will spend half their time at the site. |
| size | The equipment ranges in (scope, size, extent) from module cards to system components. |
| cost | The (economics, cost, finances) of the project was higher than projected. |
| ways of | This section explains some (approaches to, ways of) retrieving citations. |
| plan | We offer an aggressive management (plan, philosophy). |

| | |
|---|---|
| persons | Find out if all interested (parties, persons, individuals) know of the delay. |
| usefulness | The attenuators increase the (utility, usefulness) of the test instruments. |
| start | At the (inception, start) of the mission, all men will work full time on planning. |
| need for | The (requirement of, need for) high fields in the emitter barrier raises many problems. |
| end | The transmitter sends an end-of-signal message at the (end, completion) of each transmission. |
| values (characteristics) | The (values, parameters) of the equivalent circuit limit the information bandwidth. |
| changes | Since we made these (modifications, changes) our files have been up to date. |
| At the end | (Upon completion, At the end) of the warmup period, press the start button. |
| differences | We will then explain how (variations, differences) in composition affect the wavelength. |
| values | Note that the raw (parameters, values) are refined by preprocessing and normalizing. |
| change | In thin films, two factors cause the (change, deviation) in resistance. |

Simplify the italicized words in the following sentences by deleting part of the word; the word "within," for example, might have "with" or "in" removed from it, whichever fits the sentence. "Preventative examination" becomes "Preventative examination."

## SIMPLIFY ITALICIZED WORDS

| | |
|---|---|
| within | Maintenance information is *within* Volume III. |
| Depress | *Depress* the following push buttons: |
| herein (or: in this contract.) | Notify the contractor when you ship the items listed *herein*. |
| within or within (or: on the target.) | Derive these pulses at points of contrast *within* the target. |

| | |
|---|---|
| preventative | These tests are the final part of the *preventative* maintenance routine. |

Remove letters from the following italicized words; then revise the word slightly, usually adding "s." For example, "symbology" becomes "symbol[s]."

| | |
|---|---|
| leaks | We detected no other *leakage*. |
| meters | A transistor-loop current control eliminates the need for *metering*. |
| circuits (wires?) | The newer components have flexible *circuitry*. |
| symbols | Use the following *symbology*. |
| packages | The data-processor *packaging* range from module cards to system components. |
| experiments | Paragraph 5 describes the proposed *experimentation* and our analysis. |

Remove some letters from one of the following italicized words; then delete the other italicized words.

| | |
|---|---|
| except | The results are similar *with the exception* that predetection combining lowers the threshold. |
| except | The circuits of the positive and the negative signal batteries are identical *with an exception* for polarity. |

## 11-2  Circumlocutions

*Circumlocution* is the use of more words than needed, as in writing "is not the case" instead of "is false." A short expression is in parentheses in the frames below. It can replace a longer expression in the problem sentence. Circle that longer expression. When reviewing, note how the string of words in the circumlocution diffuses the message impact.

*CIRCLE THE CIRCUMLOCUTION*

| | |
|---|---|
| Through the course of each day by several periodic observations | Through the course of each day by several periodic observations, check that all indicator lamps can light. (Several times daily) |

| | |
|---|---|
| remaining-to-be-accomplished | The scheduling department then concentrates on the remaining-to-be-accomplished elements of the project. (unfinished) |
| missing from | The electronic logic operates even though the sixth envelope is missing from under the scanner. (not) |
| only at the expense of higher | These changes take off 2 pounds, but only at the expense of higher cost of production. (increase the) |
| fail to | The electron might still fail to be collected. (not) |
| is not the same | The absorption edge is not the same from crystal to crystal. (changes) |
| along the lines of | The new concentrations are along the lines of the old. (like) |
| increased by 2 to 1 | This additional reflectivity increased by 2 to 1 the light-gathering capability. (doubled) |
| in conjunction with each other | These two logic networks work in conjunction with each other. (together) |
| are the same as (those of) | The characteristics of the printed conductors are the same as those of the line. (match) |
| for a much more attractive | In short, these new techniques increase performance for a much more attractive price. (and lower the) |
| improved heat transfer from | The air flow improved heat transfer from the pump. (cooled) |
| is within | The resolution of the cathode ray tube is within these requirements. (satisfies) |
| slowness to rapid change | This slowness to rapid change arises from the weight. (inertia) |
| give much freedom from | Dry-reed switches give much freedom from cross talk and impulse noise. (greatly reduce) |
| not developing good | The gold was not developing good electric contacts. (developing poor) |
| made air surveys impossible | Smoke and haze from jungle fires made air surveys impossible. (prevented air surveys) |
| so that leaks do not occur | It waterproofs the material so that leaks do not occur. (, preventing leaks) |

| | |
|---|---|
| programming in early stages of development | We will not use programming in early stages of development. (undeveloped programming) |

## 11-3  Vague Words

Vague words or overly general ones carry multiple meanings. They are highly useful to introduce broad subjects. But they should not be used where more specific, concrete words can be used. "Simple," for example, is perfectly useful in many contexts but is too general a word if what you mean is "with fewer parts" or "easy to design." Similarly, avoid a broad expression like "is economical" if you mean "costs less to make (buy, design, maintain)." Fad words, because of their overuse, come to mean almost anything. "Environment," for example, is used in place of exact words like "weather," "climate," "humidity," "mud," "wind," "in space," "under water," and even "truck." Similarly, "atmosphere" is used in place of the exact "air."

### Vague Nouns

Inside the parentheses of the following sentences are an overly general noun and a more precise noun. Among them are nouns such as the following:

"vehicle" with more specific words such as: "truck," "automobile," etc.
"document" or "publication" with "book," "report," or "pamphlet"
"facility" or "site" with "building," "factory," "laboratory," "office," etc.
"equipment" with "drills," "lathes," "tachometer," etc.
"producing" or "working" with "designing," or "engineering"
"making" or "preparing," with "depositing," or "sandpapering."

Circle the specific word in the parentheses of the following sentences. Always include the rejected words when you review each frame. Avoid using general nouns unless their generality is appropriate to the context.

*CIRCLE THE MORE SPECIFIC WORD*

| | |
|---|---|
| manual | This (publication, manual, literature) explains how to operate the equipment at the following sites. |
| trucks | These (vehicles, trucks) are now being prepared for shipment. |
| designing | We have begun (designing, achieving) the breadboard model. |

| report | We have drafted a (report, document, publication) on how sheet resistance affects high-speed performance. |
| Designing | (Producing, Designing) circuit boards takes many steps. |
| laboratory | We will do the research at our (facility, site, laboratory) in Flourtown, Pennsylvania. |
| research | This subsidy also financed (work, efforts, research) at the University of Geneva. |
| enlargers | The photographic (facilities, enlargers) in our plant cannot handle larger boards. |
| engineers | This department has its own full-time (engineers, individuals) solving character-recognition problems. |
| Pressing | (Operating, Working, Pressing) this push button starts the analyzer. |
| office | The operations (area, office, place) controls communications. |
| air conditioners | These (units, entities, air conditioners) will be in the wall. |
| equipment | To summarize, for carrying out these experiments, our company has a strong combination of experienced men and (facilities, equipment). |
| depositing | We use evaporation extensively in (preparing, depositing) thin films on glass. |
| at normal air temperatures | The coil maintains the operating temperatures (under normal atmospheric conditions, at normal air temperatures). |

### Vague Verbs

In the following frames are some overly general verbs. "Added" in the following sentence, for example, is so vague it gives just a general drift:

**We** *added* **a capacitor across the coil.**

The specific meaning could probably be given by one of the following verbs:

**We** {connected / wired / soldered} **a capacitor across the coil.**

"Covers" in the following sentence similarly hints only vaguely at what the volume does:

**This volume** *covers* **the development and fabrication of display kits.**

The volume might be doing one of the following:

**This volume** {
**criticizes**
**studies** } **the development and fabrication of . . .**
**analyzes**
**explains how display kits are developed and. . . .**
**discusses how to develop and fabricate. . . .**

Other unnecessarily general verbs with possible replacements are:

"fastened" instead of the more precise "welded," or "bolted"
"implement" instead of the more precise "manufacture," or "start"
"finalize" instead of the more precise "sign," or "agree to"
"developed" and }
  "accomplished" } instead of the more precise "engineered," or "designed"
"determine" instead of the more precise "learn," "set," or "fix"
"deals with" instead of the more precise "explains," "describes," or "shows how to"
"affects," or }
  "alters" } instead of the more precise "increase," or "decrease."

Circle the most specific of the verbs in parentheses in the following sentences. While checking left, note the imprecision of the remaining verbs.

## CIRCLE THE MOST EXACT VERB

| | |
|---|---|
| lights | The concentrator (indicates, evidences, lights) at overflow capacity. |
| lists | Table 13A (manifests, lists) the location of each power supply. |
| fly | The other pilots will (operate, fly, run) the plane. |
| sounds | The second alarm (occurs, sounds, takes place) whenever the power output reaches dangerous values. |
| describes | This report (is concerned with, deals with, describes) ways of varying the absorption in cesium vapor. |

| means that | "Correction by replacement" (is when, means that, signifies that) duplicate spares replace major modules. |
| --- | --- |
| designed | Our company next (designed, accomplished) a vertical pantograph. |
| increase; increased | The temperature (increase, alteration) should have (increased, altered) the vapor pressure. |
| learned | We (learned, determined, ascertained) the best level by experiment. |
| describes | This booklet (considers, deals with, describes) the equipment at the control station only. |
| increases | This structure (increases, affects, alters) the possibility of reducing the weight. |
| starts | The clock pulse (accomplishes, achieves, starts) the read in. |
| ensures | Our company (approaches, ensures, cultivates) reliability as follows: |
| learned | He (determined, learned, resolved) the lattice parameters of the first crystals by x-ray analyses. |
| explains | This section (explains, develops, involves) the quantitative performance values of the concrete beams. |
| operated | The air gap is the distance between the armature and the heel piece when the relay is (operated, performed). |
| fix | Those findings will help us (determine, fix, establish) the allowable leeway. |
| designed | The J. Pommer Company has already (implemented, accomplished, designed) the lock valve. |
| engineering | We are now (configuring, fashioning, engineering) the air compressor. |
| is operating | This kind of extensometer already (is implemented, is operating). |

| find | First you have to (establish, determine, find) the correct ratio. |
| --- | --- |
| measured | They (determined, measured, appraised) the thickness of each layer with an interference monitor. |

## 11-4  Repeating Words for Clarity and Force

Many times, writers develop ponderous styles because they fear repeating a word within a certain number of sentences. They seek out new and unusual words, often using ones that do not fit the context. Robert Louis Stevenson is often quoted against repetition. "The one rule," said Stevenson, "is to be infinitely various: monotony of any sort displeases and repels the reader."

Where immediacy is primary, as in technical prose, you can subordinate this excellent advice to Stevenson's own exception: He says: "Any repetition *except what is necessary for clearness and force* wearies [the reader]."

Be infinitely various in writing novels and personal essays. But in your technical exposition be clear and forceful. When that forces you to repeat words, do so. If you call something a console, don't later call it a cabinet, then a case, then a desk. If you start out calling something a routine, don't later call it a method or a technique. Select a fitting word and stick to it. You will only confuse your readers with new words.

The problem sentences below use two different expressions to convey the same thought. For example, the following sentence uses the indefinite "handles" to avoid repeating a form of "rounding off."

**"The** *rounding-off* **routine** *handles* **(rounds off) fractions."**

Choose the more precise expression, and write it in place of the other. They are usually in italics.

*REPEAT THE MORE PRECISE EXPRESSION*

| cost | Some *cost* thousands of dollars, while others *are priced in the range of* millions. |
| --- | --- |
| types (or "groups") | Of the ten *types* of phonemes, he could recognize only five *groups* by their formant locations. |
| was too high (possibly: . . . had to be reduced) | Damage to letters *was too high;* also the number of double letters fed past the scanner *had to be reduced.* |

| | |
|---|---|
| "Links" is probably more precise, but either might do. | Twenty-four channel *links* can use these frequencies, while sixty channel *systems* can use the other. |
| this commercial equipment (or: . . . we can use it) | We have specified *commercial equipment* because we can use *this material* for training and for spares. |
| Either. | The transmitter *has a density of* 3,315 pounds per cubic foot; the amplifier power supply *is* 20 pounds per cubic foot. |
| Either. ("Chosen," if choosing is important) | The word "Mary" *was chosen as* the all-voiced word; the word "vipers" *is* the word containing voiced and unvoiced fricatives. |
| signal to the trunk line (or: This signal) | The receiver sends a *signal to the trunk line* to start sending addresses. The *trunk-line signal* stops when the receiver register accepts the first digit of the address. |
| are connected | This section explains how the inputs *are connected* to the wafer. It describes only one segment of the wafer, since inputs to the other segments *operate* similarly. |
| the radar set (better: the set; or: it) | The accuracy of the data from *the radar set depends on the quality of maintenance the equipment* gets. |
| Either. | We will use field-tested programming *techniques,* shunning undeveloped *methods.* |
| guarantee | In addition to *guaranteeing* that no signal components are lost (which clipped-differentiated speech does not *do*), the inversion removes harmonic distortion. |
| Either. | The audible alarm strikes only once *for* equipment changes or *when* equipment switches. |

## 11-5 Unclear Referents for "This," "These," and "Which"

Pronouns such as "it," "they," "these," and "which" are useful to avoid repeating words. However, they cause ambiguity when their referent—what is not being repeated—is not clear. For example, "they" in the following sentence has two possible referents:

*The circuit boards* **will be put in** *the modules* **when** *they* **are dry.**

The reference can be made unmistakeable by repeating it:

**The circuit boards will be put in the modules when** *the circuit boards* **(or** *the modules***) are dry.**

The italicized expressions in the following sentences can similarly be taken to refer to two referents.

## REVISE WITH THE MOST LIKELY REFERENT

| | |
|---|---|
| if the wire (component) is insulated | A printed wire can run below a component if *it* is insulated. |
| whether the station (the call) is active. | How a station answers a call depends on whether *it* is active or inactive. |
| which switch (or: This switch) | The speed can be selected at a switch on the control panel, *which* energizes a clutch. |
| for which light (or: for which axis) | The darker image came from light polarized parallel to the C axis, for *which* the absorption edge appears deeper in the red end of the spectrum. |
| from which tabulation | The computer will analyze the information and tabulate it according to how often the events combine, *from which* we will choose the best decision levels for each phoneme. |
| This type of antenna (possibly: this radiation pattern) | A vertical half-wave dipole antenna develops the desired radiation pattern. *This* presents a problem at low frequencies. |
| This gating circuit (or: This noise removal; or: Both are described in) | To remove the noise, you can use an ac bias, or a separate gating circuit. *This* is described in Appendix C. |
| These problems. These high fields | Tunnel injection raised several problems relating to high fields in the emitter barrier. *These* induced investigators to study other methods. |
| This short circuit (possibly: This channel shift) | The input and output lines short-circuit whenever the channels shift. *This* deletes the stored information. |

| This filter(ing) (removal) stops (Not: This frequency stops) | The filter removes the residual carrier frequency. *This* stops undesirable feedback through the precession coils. |
| This overlap (or: This arrangement) | Delays in the clock-pulse distribution system are arranged so that data pulses always overlap clock pulses. *This feature* eliminates spikes or sneak pulses. |

COMMENT: AS OBSERVED EARLIER, YOU SHOULD AVOID UNCOMMON TECHNICAL TERMS. BUT WHEN THEY ARE NECESSARY YOU CAN EXPLAIN THEM IN AN APPOSITIVE:

At its apogee, *that is, the highest point of its trajectory,* the missile still. . . .

OR YOU CAN EXPLAIN THE TERM IN PARENTHESES:

THE LOX (liquid oxygen) is then. . . .

## 11-6 Review

### CIRCLE THE SIMPLER, MORE SPECIFIC WORD

| job | The input-output register does the same (function, job) while testing as while loading. |
| study | This problem has been under serious (study, consideration) for over 100 years. |
| men | These planes will transport (personnel, individuals, men) between sites. |
| change | The temperature (variation, change, alteration) should have doubled the cesium vapor pressure. |
| design | The modular (concept, design) reduces the number of spares. |
| plan (principle) | This (plan, axiom, philosophy) of 100 percent backup extends to the automatic switching equipment, the voice multiplex, and the power amplifier. |
| type | Each (category, type, classification) of subscriber equipment offers different benefits. |

Simplify the following italicized words by removing some letters and, where necessary, rewriting the word.

## SIMPLIFY THE ITALICIZED WORDS

| | |
|---|---|
| Press (Push) | *Depress* the red push button until the red light goes out. |
| in | Voltages *within* this cabinet are dangerous. |
| except | These tests apply to all equipment at this site *with the exception* as noted. |
| in (possibly, with) | No classified material appears *within* this series. |
| except | All equipment *with the exception of* the power amplifier is in one van. |
| preventative | The *preventative* maintenance schedule was set up by the design engineer. |
| expenses | Explain excessive *expenditures* in the remarks section. |
| in a vacuum | Many III-V compound semiconductors dissociate readily when heated *in vacuo.* (Don't use Latin where English would do.) |

COMMENT: BECAUSE ITS TERMS ARE VAGUE AND OVERLOADED, THE FOLLOWING SENTENCE SAYS NOT MUCH MORE THAN THAT SOMETHING IS OK:

Some *practical cases* are *more optimum* and easier to *deal* with.

"CASES" AND "DEAL WITH" CAN USUALLY BE REPLACED WITH SPECIFIC, CONCRETE WORDS. THE REDUNDANT "MORE OPTIMUM" WAS INTENDED TO MEAN SOMETHING LIKE "BETTER," THOUGH IT SUGGESTS MUCH MORE. THE WRITER ACTUALLY INTENDED THE CONCRETE STATEMENT:

Some tests are easier to set up and to evaluate.

## CIRCLE THE MORE PRECISE WORD

| | |
|---|---|
| design | We have begun (design, efforts) on a phase modulator that will generate continuous beat frequencies. |
| booklet | This (booklet, document, publication) discusses the following: |

| | |
|---|---|
| run | The subroutines in a computer program must be (run, implemented, accomplished) first. |
| fixes | The field at which the electron cloud begins to generate optical phonons (determines, fixes) the limiting velocity for carriers. |
| handbooks | Our (publications, handbooks, documents) are not clearly written. |
| set up | We recommend that you (implement, set up, occasion) a more reliable system. |
| Pressing | (Operating, Pressing, Working on) this push button activates all solenoids in the low-voltage circuits. |
| less | The evaporation rate was held to (less, better) than 1 percent. |
| factory | Appendix C describes this (facility, factory). |
| describe | The tables (contain information relative to, involve, describe) the equipment. |
| learn | We will (learn, determine) the least feasible thickness by studying likely materials. |
| engineering | We have a solid background for (working on, engineering, advising on) card readers. |
| increases | Flash evaporation (widens the scope of, increases, proliferates) the semiconductors that can be deposited. |
| shaped | We doubt that precise and uniformly directed fields can be (the case, shaped, accomplished) with permanent magnets. |
| temperature | The air blower helps maintain tuning despite changes in (environmental conditions, temperature). |
| false | This has proved (not to be the case, false). |
| means that | "Correction by repair" (is when, obtains when, means that) spares replace the faulty part. |

Repeat the most precise and simple expression. Watch for italics.

## REVISE, REPEATING FOR CLARITY

| | |
|---|---|
| structure | The crystalline *nature* of the deposit depends on the *structure* of the substrate. |
| A simple design (or: This design; It) | A *simple design* is necessary in equipment that has to operate in sand and rain. *This feature* also reduces the cost of quantity production. |
| cabinets | The *cabinets* will be like similar Signal Corps *equipment*. |
| This lack (of speaker identification) | This device has a word-articulation rate of 95 percent but lacks high-quality speaker identification. *This problem* can be solved by using the circuit described in Figure 2. |
| This poor development (This poor contact) | Gold developed a poor electrical contact. *This* will be remedied by a technique used in laser diodes. |
| To conform to these prices, | We are proud of our history of conforming to contract prices. To do *this,* we laid down stringent controls. |

COMMENT: THOUGH YOU SHOULD USE AS FEW WORDS AS YOU CAN, DON'T CONSTRICT YOUR WRITING SO THAT YOU END UP WITH ABYSMALLY VAGUE TERMS—SUCH AS "FINANCIAL EXPERIENCE" IN THE FOLLOWING SENTENCE:

This table shows our company's *financial experience* on three major nuclear power stations.

SINCE "FINANCIAL EXPERIENCE" MEANS SOMETHING LIKE "EXPERIENCE WITH MONEY," IT IS OBVIOUS THAT NO TABLE COULD SHOW THAT FOR ANY COMPANY THAT HAD LASTED FOR MORE THAN A FEW DAYS. WHAT THE TABLE DID SHOW IS WHAT THE WRITER SHOULD HAVE WRITTEN:

This table shows that our company's final costs on . . . stations were close to contract costs.

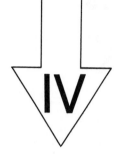

# STRESSING WHAT IS IMPORTANT

The following chapters deal with factors that change sentence emphasis, showing how you can bring out the emphasis you want. Among the factors dealt with are forms that play up the subject while downgrading its activity, highly personal forms and overly impersonal ones, overburdened modifiers, and punctuation. In much of this you will continue removing deadwood, developing dynamic verbs, and lightening sentences.

# RELEASING VERBS: ELIMINATING "IT" AND "THERE"

"It" and "there" dissipate verb power—often unnecessarily—by stressing other sentence elements, usually subjects. "Could" and "would" distract from the immediacy of the verb activity by recalling conditions that must be fulfilled before the verb activity can happen.

## 12-1  Anticipatory Words

"It" and "there" as anticipatory words focus attention on the words immediately following them. In the following sentence "it is" directs attention to "this necessity":

*It is* **this necessity** *that* **adds to their complexity.**

"It is" also deemphasizes the verb "adds." Where such deemphasis is not fitting, it should be changed to give the verb full play, thus:

~~It is~~ **This necessity** ~~that~~ **adds to their complexity.**

Make similar deletions in the following problem sentences. Before checking left, reread the sentence to be sure you have removed all unnecessary words, such as "that" in the example sentence.

DELETE "IT," "THERE," AND ACCOMPANYING WORDS

~~there is~~ . . . ~~that~~          There is a flywheel on the drive shaft that en-
                                     sures a constant speed.

147

COMMENT: WHEN REVIEWING THESE SENTENCES, NOTE THE CHANGE IN EMPHASIS – FROM THE SUBJECT IN THE ORIGINAL SENTENCE (IN THE PRECEDING SENTENCE, "A FLYWHEEL") TO ITS ACTIVITY IN THE REVISION.

| | |
|---|---|
| (There was) . . . (that) | There was no other computer that could match its capacity. |
| (There are) . . . (that) | There are two enormous boilers that heat the entire station. |
| (there are) . . . (that) | For this conversion, there are eight steps that must be carried out. |
| (It is) . . . (which) | It is the envelope detection of these combined signals which develops the demodulated video output. |

## 12-2  Changes to the Stressed Word

In the following problem sentences you will have to rewrite slightly the word emphasized by the anticipatory word:

**It is** *obvious* **that such cannot be done.**

becomes:

**Obvious*ly*, such cannot be done.**

### REWRITE WITHOUT "IT" OR "THERE"

| | |
|---|---|
| Clear*ly* from the averages, they. . . . | It is clear from the averages that they preferred the four-bit system slightly over the V-T system. |
| Eviden*tly* the time needed to. . . . | It is evident that the time needed to search for all possible targets is still too long. |
| Interesting*ly*, the electron-phonon. . . . | It is interesting to note that the electron-phonon process does not influence the electron-attenuation lengths. ("To note" becomes superfluous.) |
| Since . . . , obvious*ly*, we are not. . . . | Since the radar sets can detect targets up to 18,000 meters, it is obvious that we are not using their full capability. |

| | |
|---|---|
| Possibly, diffused electrodes will. . . . | The possibility exists that diffused electrodes will improve the breakdown strength. (i.e., It is a possibility that diffused electrodes will improve. . . .) |

## 12-3 Changed Word Not Necessary

Though they sometimes add an intended emphasis, expressions such as those developed in the preceding sentences are often unnecessary and should be removed. If the message were so clear or obvious, the sentence would not have to be written.

In most of the following sentences the "-ly" word is not necessary. Take it out. But do not remove it where it is necessary.

### DELETE UNNECESSARY "-LY" WORDS ONLY

| | |
|---|---|
| (evidently) | Thus, *evidently*, the time needed to search for all possible targets is long. |
| (obviously) | Since the radar sets can detect targets up to 18,000 meters away, obviously their full capability is not being used. |
| (obviously) | Obviously, the composition and the thickness of these films are of primary importance. |
| No deletion. | Possibly, diffuse electrons will improve the breakdown strength. (Note that only a possibility is being asserted.) |
| (Interestingly) (Possibly leave in—depending on intent.) | Interestingly, electron-attenuator lengths are not influenced by the electron-phonon process. |
| (Clearly) | Clearly, from all the averages the four-bit system was preferred slightly over the V-T system. |
| No deletion. | Apparently, from the experiments just described, these graphs are faulty. (Note that the fault is only apparent.) |
| (Clearly) | Clearly, it is best to use these bits to encode the amplitude values. |

## 12-4   Moving the Subject

After you remove "it" and "there" from the following sentences, move the main subject to precede the verb. For example, to delete "there" from:

(There) are only 110 bits of information derived during each sampling period.

Move the subject to precede "are derived":

(There) are only 110 bits of information derived during each sampling period. (Only 110 bits of information are derived during. . . .)

In the following sentences use arrows (as above) to show the new location of the subject.

### REWRITE WITHOUT "IT" OR "THERE"

| | |
|---|---|
| (There) was no airplane available. (No airplane was available.) | (There) was no airplane available. |
| (There) remains another dehumidifier as a replacement. (Another dehumidifier remains. . . .) | There remains another dehumidifier as a replacement. |
| (There) is a sixty-channel . . . subsystem in the. . . . (A sixty-channel transportable subsystem is in the. . . .) | There is a sixty-channel transportable subsystem in the communications system. |
| (There) were some objections voiced during the. . . . (Some objections were voiced. . . .) | There were some objections voiced during the ninety-minute hearing. |
| (It) is clearly the best choice to use these bits. . . . (Clearly, the best choice is to. . . .) | It is clearly the best choice to use these bits in encoding the amplitude values. |

## 12-5   Gerund Subjects instead of Infinitives

Revise the following sentences similarly. The subjects will be infinitives. Thus:

*It* was easy to study.

will become:

*To study* was easy.

Change this infinitive subject to a gerund ("-ing" form):

**Study*ing* was easy.**

---

## *REWRITE WITHOUT "IT"*

| | |
|---|---|
| Learning the new procedures was easy. | ~~It~~ was easy to learn the new procedures. |
| | ~~To learn~~ Learning the new |
| Getting transportable equipment is difficult. | It is difficult to get transportable equipment. |
| Packaging equipment for transportation is difficult. | It is difficult to package equipment for transportation. |
| | Packaging |
| Extracting the individual formants has been difficult and complicated. | It has been difficult and complicated to extract the individual formants. |

## 12-6  Rewriting the Verbs

After moving the subject in the following sentences, slightly recast the verb.

---

## *REWRITE WITHOUT "IT" OR "THERE"*

| | |
|---|---|
| Earlier research has firmly established that. . . . | *It has been firmly established by* earlier research that this circuit will improve the signal-to-noise ratio. |
| | Earlier research has |
| The four-bit system was preferred slightly over the. . . . | There was a slight preference for the four-bit system over the V-T system. |
| | The four-bit system was _____ slightly |
| . . . only when the polarity of the input signal changes. | The logic reverses itself only when there is a change in the polarity of the input signal. (Make active voice) |
| | . . . only when the polarity of the. . . . |
| Demand continues that. . . . | *There is a continued demand* that we reduce the bandwidth requirement. |
| | Demand _____ that we reduce. . . . (Keep present tense and active voice.) |

| | |
|---|---|
| This manual is not intended to re-place. . . . | It is not the intent of this manual to replace applicable military\specifications.<br><br>This manual is not⌐ |
| This paper shows that. . . . | In this paper it is shown that this technique can form active all-film triodes.<br><br>This paper |
| Reflections can be excessive, un-less. . . . | There can be excessive reflections unless the printed conductors match the lines.<br><br>Reflections |
| Vendors must be selected care-fully. | There must be careful selection of vendors.<br><br>Vendors must |
| Much smaller and lighter power supplies are now available. | There are now available much smaller and lighter power supplies.<br><br>. . . power supplies |
| A study of these chords is needed. (or: . . . should be studied.) | There is need for a study of these chords.<br><br>A study of |
| Letters were damaged at four points along their path of travel. | There were four points along their path of travel at which letters were damaged.<br><br>Letters were damaged at |

## 12-7 Verb-muffling Expression in the Body of a Sentence

The stifling expressions in the preceding sentences were usually among the first words in the sentence. They are in the body of the following sentences, as in:

**The conclusions (that were) drawn from this research are summarized below.**

When reviewing each sentence, note both the interrupted flow in the original and the change in emphasis between the original and the revised version.

*DELETE VERB-MUFFLING EXPRESSIONS*

| | |
|---|---|
| (that was) | The code system that was selected was the single-network system. |

| | |
|---|---|
| (which is) | He already had described past research which is directly relevant to our own. |
| (that are) | Automatic voltage regulators that are insensitive to 10 percent changes in input voltage stabilize the power. |
| (it is) | Where it is needed, we will include convertors on tie lines. |
| (it was) | As it was mentioned above, such a miscibility gap appears in the quasi-binary phosphide-antimony system. |
| (which are) | All the compounds which are described here belong to the five-component system Ga:In:P:As:Sb. |
| (what are) | Two new amplifiers are what are needed. |
| (there) (or: A switch for . . . follows the . . .) | Following the low-pass filter there is a switch for transferring the R-F output. |
| (those) | The reports we will turn in are those listed in the contract. |

Remove "that are" expressions from the following sentences. Then interchange the words around the deletion.

### DELETE "THAT ARE" AND REWRITE

| | |
|---|---|
| Operating sets develop a faint whirr. | Sets that are operating develop a faint whirr. Operating sets |
| Defective indicator lamps remain dark. | Indicator lamps that are defective remain dark. Defective |
| . . . other relevant criteria. | The technician must set up other *criteria that are relevant.* . . . must set up other |
| . . . stations raise varied and difficult problems. | Transportable stations raise *problems that are varied and difficult.* |
| . . . free carriers were absorbed. | Wherever the beam fell *there was absorption of free carriers.* |

## 12-8  Suppressed Conditionals

"Could" and "would" direct attention to conditions that must be fulfilled before verb activity can take place. Limit this subjunctive function. For one thing, don't use it unless it is important that you refer to the condition. Make positive statements wherever you can. Rather than an "iffy" statement such as:

**The processor** *could work* **with different types of radar sets.**

Make a positive assertion:

**This processor** *can work* (*works*) **with different types. . . .**

If you consider what is the unexpressed (suppressed) condition for the original sentence, you will see why it should not even have been alluded to, for it is the wholly obvious necessity that the processor be connected to the sets: "If the processor were to be connected to the radar sets, it would. . . ."

This brings us to the second reason for limiting references to antecedent conditions: if you use many of them, you create an uncertain, tentative tone, which keeps readers mentally backtracking to the condition. The present assertion gets hidden behind the antecedents.

This is especially true in proposals, where the positive message of entire volumes becomes enmeshed in ever-present—and often unwritten—"if's." The all-embracing condition "If this proposal were to be accepted, our company would do. . . ." soon mingles with subordinate conditions—also often unwritten—about the subject of the proposal, such as, "If the proposed equipment were to be switched on, it would do. . . ." This then gets mired in sub-subordinate conditions relating to the equipment, such as what happens if optional parts are used or at different gauge settings.

As with the passive voice, keep in mind that this subjunctive function is highly useful. It is not its use but its overuse and its misuse that is at fault. Use it where it carries the necessary message. But where you can do so, avoid this suggestion of antecedent conditions. Simply change "could" to "can" and "would" to "will."

*REPLACE "COULD" WITH "CAN"*

can
could                     We could easily make such an oscilloscope.

COMMENT: WHEN REVIEWING THESE SENTENCES, NOTICE THE "IFFY" TONE OF THE "-OULD" SENTENCE—ARISING FROM ITS IMPLICATION OF A CONDITION THAT MUST BE FULFILLED.

can
could                    A single equivalent sound could replace any vowel sound.

| | |
|---|---|
| can <br> ~~could~~ | We could develop a faster device. |
| can be steered <br> ~~could be steered~~ | The truck could be steered from either front or rear. |

Often you can change the conditional "would" to the future "will." Usually, however, you will find it best to rewrite the verb with neither "would" nor "will," changing, for example, the tentative:

**Continuous operation** *would cause* **a printout of a nonsort code.**

to the assertive:

**Continuous operation** *will cause* (*causes*) **a printout of a. . . .**

When you review these frames, note how the "-ould" words glance to the condition.

## REWRITE WITHOUT "WOULD" (WHERE POSSIBLE, WITHOUT "WILL")

| | |
|---|---|
| means (will mean) <br> ~~would mean~~ | Unnecessary complexity *would mean* increased size, weight, and cost. |
| combines (will combine) <br> ~~would combine~~ | Another method of encoding would combine the symbols into arbitrary groups of three. |
| causes (will cause) <br> ~~would cause~~ | Continuous operation would cause a printout. |
| is (will be) <br> ~~would be~~ | The one-bit system would be simpler to produce. |

## REPLACE "COULD" OR "WOULD" WITH "CAN" OR "WILL," OR REWRITE THE VERB WITHOUT "WOULD"

| | |
|---|---|
| can <br> ~~could~~ | This enables the main start switch; you could now start the machine. |
| appears     can <br> ~~would appear~~ . . ~~could~~ be developed. | Since the decay is exponential, it would appear that a faster device could be developed. <br><br> (There are two.) |
| seems to offer (? offers) <br> ~~would seem to offer~~ | Thermionic injection would seem to offer the highest collection efficiencies. |
| can <br> ~~could~~ be replaced | Any multiple-formant vowel sound could be replaced by a single equivalent sound. |

| | |
|---|---|
| can ~~could~~ construct | We could construct a smaller centrifuge for remote locations. |
| caused (will cause) ~~would cause~~ | The impact would cause the assembly to travel. |

COMMENT: "COULD" AND "WOULD" ARE ESPECIALLY HARMFUL IN SALES LITERATURE. THEIR UNCERTAIN TONE UNDERMINES THE OFFERING, AS IN THE TENTATIVE:

The heater would provide 30,000 BTU's.

WHICH COULD BE THE POSITIVE:

The heater provides (will provide). . . .

EVEN MORE DAMAGING, HOWEVER, IS THAT, SINCE THE CONDITION IS NOT GIVEN, THE READER CAN SUPPLY HIS OWN. HE CAN PLAYFULLY SUPPOSE IT TO BE WHATEVER HE WANTS TO, SUCH AS,

If the heater were to work, it would provide. . . .

OR

If it were possible to light it, it would provide. . . .

MORE ASSERTIVE STATEMENTS AVOID THIS POSSIBILITY.


## 12-9 Review

You do not have to rewrite the following sentences. Just delete unnecessary expressions.

### DELETE "IT," "THERE," "THAT," AND SIMILAR EXPRESSIONS

| | |
|---|---|
| ~~which is~~ | The intercept operator removes the tape from the perforator, then inserts it into a reader which is connected to a typing perforator. |
| ~~It is~~ . . . ~~that~~ | It is for this reason that we suggest the alternative program. |
| , ~~which are~~ | This reliability accords with the CCIT recommendations, which are listed in another section. |
| ~~There are~~ . . . ~~that~~ | There are other preprocessing techniques that can simplify extraction. |
| ~~there~~ | Were there any exceptions taken to the agreement? |

| | |
|---|---|
| (that is) | Only one company manufactures the delay circuit that is needed for the new model. |
| (that of) | The technique used is *that of* vacuum evaporation. |
| (There are) . . (that) | There are four parallel branch currents that flow through V-1. |
| (There are) . . (which) . . (which) | There are two identical front panels which act as card carriers and which contain the fixed contacts. |
| (It is) . . (that) | It is this necessity that adds to the complexity of the simulator. |
| (There are) . . (that) | There are many applications that make this device useful for speech analysis. |
| (what) he (was doing) was | Today we would say that what he was doing was interpreting the criteria. |
| (that the) . . (is) (or, (that)) | A meter reading means *that the* trouble *is* in the circuit following tube V1. |
| (If there is) . . (it) (that the) . . (is) | *If there is* a meter reading, *it* means *that the* trouble *is* in the circuit following tube V1. (This is the preceding sentence as originally written.) |
| (what) . . . (is) | In cross modulation *what* this result amounts to *is* the failure of these circuits. |
| (With reference to) . . (they) | With reference to the instructions they must be followed exactly. |
| that are (other relevant manuals) | This table references other manuals that are relevant. (Shift words slightly.) |

## REPLACE "-OULD" WORDS WITH "CAN" OR "WILL," OR REVISE THE VERB WITHOUT "WOULD." CHECK LEFT

| | |
|---|---|
| will interrupt (interrupt) (would interrupt) | These short-term variations would interrupt voice communications very little. |
| will cause (causes) (would cause) | The continuous operation of the logic would cause a nonsort code to be printed. |
| can (could) install | We could install standby devices to measure this pressure. |

| | |
|---|---|
| can operate (operates)<br>(could) operate | We delivered a 600-channel, range-gated processor that could operate with many types of radar sets. |
| will<br>(would) then be continued.<br>(It will then continue.) | This study should be well advanced when the proposed program begins. It *would* then be continued. (Make active in voice.) |
| are (will be, were)<br>(would be) | At growth rates higher than 10 angstroms a second, some of the lighter particles would be blown away from the evaporator. |
| will be (are)<br>(would be) needed | Since the dry-reed relays operate once a call and about 100 times a day, 55 years would be needed for $2 \times 10^7$ operations. |
| need (will need)<br>(would need) . .<br>needs (will need)<br>(would need) | With Faro coding, three of the symbols would need two binary digits; the other symbol would need three.<br>(There are two.) |

# BEING PERSONAL OR BEING IMPERSONAL

Both overly personal and highly impersonal styles can emphasize aspects that distract from the main message. Also, impersonal writing relies heavily on the passive voice, with all its weaknesses. And personal writing fosters deadwood, usually verbs.

## 13-1 Writing about People

When fitting, feel free to write about people. You will help your readers relate to what you are saying. Forget the superstition that scientific objectivity demands impersonal writing. The scientist's writing style does not make his work objective. His technique and his findings do that. If similar techniques can validate his findings, there is objectivity. But for this validation he must convey precise information, describing clearly what he has done and found. Since he can sometimes do this best by writing about human beings, he should—and does—write about them. Readers can more readily picture persons acting than events that just happen without anyone doing anything.

So use the names of people; write about "our engineers," "we," and "you." And even use "I"—where it is accurate and fitting and not just egocentric display.

### People Mentioned in the Sentence

The following problem sentences, while passive in voice, do refer to people, but the people underplay their role. Rewrite the sentences in the active voice. Change, for example, "The findings were studied by the engineer" to "The engineer studied the findings." When reviewing, note the increased directness of the more personal form.

## REWRITE IN ACTIVE VOICE

| | |
|---|---|
| Half the listeners preferred the set. . . . | The set having this logic was preferred by *half the listeners.* <br> Half the listeners |
| Professor L. Mancini made the measurements. . . . | The measurements below were made by *Professor L. Mancini.* |
| Our engineers have shown extracting the information to be. . . . | Extracting the information has been shown by our engineers to be simple and easy. |
| Several authors have discussed the limitations on. . . . | The limitations on power from a back-biased photodiode and on its information bandwidth from the lumped-constant, equivalent-circuit parameters have been discussed by several authors. |

COMMENT: SPECIFYING WHO ACTED OFTEN GIVES IMPORTANT INFORMATION.

From these results *it was decided* that. . . .

MIGHT BE WRITTEN—IF RELEVANT—TO TELL WHO DID THE DECIDING:

The present writers (We, Our staff) decided that. . . .

SIMILARLY,

The proposed communication system includes transportable subsystems.

WHICH DOES NOT SAY WHOSE WAS THE PROPOSED SYSTEM, MIGHT BE MORE MEANINGFUL AS:

Our (Their) proposed . . . system includes. . . .

### Suggested Subjects instead of Passives

Since the following passive-voice sentences do not contain personal subjects, one is given:

## REWRITE IN ACTIVE VOICE, USING SUGGESTED SUBJECTS

| | |
|---|---|
| *We measured* the oscillator signal. . . . | The oscillator signal was measured with a voltmeter. We |
| *Our engineers feel* (that) baking increases the. . . . | Baking is felt to increase the resistance of these films. <br> Our engineers <br> (Keep the tense present.) |

| | |
|---|---|
| *Our employees installed* the new colorimeter. . . . | The new colorimeter was installed in November.<br>Our employees |
| For these reasons *we assume* (that) enough heat is. . . . | For these reasons, it is assumed that enough heat is available for the reaction.<br>For these reasons we |
| We believe (that) the resulting waveforms. . . . | It is believed that the resulting waveforms represent the true trends in perception.<br>We |
| We have completed a draft of the publication on the . . . | A draft of the publication on the effect of sheet resistance on high-speed performance has been completed.<br>We have |
| Others (have) concluded that small-carrier generation. . . . | It has been concluded that small-carrier generation discouraged feasibility studies.<br>Others |

COMMENT: THE LEGITIMACY OF PERSONAL WRITING SHOULD NOT BE TAKEN AS A LICENSE FOR EGOCENTRICITY. TECHNICAL WRITING MUST CONCENTRATE ON THE SUBJECT MATTER, NOT ON THE WRITER'S EGO. IT SHOULD NOT BECOME A VEHICLE FOR PERSONAL EXPRESSION.

NOR SHOULD THIS LEGITIMACY CONFLICT WITH LONG-FOUND ORGANIZATIONAL PRACTICES. MANY HAVE EDITORIAL POLICIES TO SHUN PERSONAL FORMS AS THE SUREST WAY TO AVOID EXTREMELY PERSONAL WRITING. WHEN WRITING FOR SUCH PUBLICATIONS, YOU CAN STILL USE EXPRESSIONS LIKE "THIS WRITER" OR "THE PRESENT WRITER(S)."

### "You" instead of "It" and "There" Passives

Addressing your readers directly as "you" relates them immediately to your message, which is especially important in instructions. The following sentences with their "it" and "there" and passives are indirect. Use "you" as the subject, and rewrite them in the active voice, so that they speak directly to the reader. For example write:

*It* **will be seen that. . . .**

with "you" as:

*You* **will see that. . . .**

Note that some of these are obviously intended as instructions, though they only hint at that by their use of "must," "should," and "have to."

## REWRITE IN ACTIVE VOICE, WITH "YOU" WRITTEN IN

| | |
|---|---|
| You will recall that ordinarily. . . . | It will be recalled that ordinarily the D$_2$ line is not recommended for optical pumping of cesium. |
| | You will |
| You will see that the. . . . | It will be seen that the clock pulse combines with nonclock time-data elements. |
| | You will |
| You can see that the. . . . | It can be seen that the pattern has sixteen transitions for thirty-two bits. |
| You should use a soft cloth. . . . | A soft cloth should be used to remove the dust. |

### Imperatives

Many sentences like the preceding are really intended as commands or directions. As such they should be written as imperatives. Sentences such as:

A soft cloth *should* be used (*You should* use a soft cloth) to remove the dust.

become imperatives as:

*Use* a soft cloth to remove. . . .

(The subject, "You," is understood in imperatives: "[You] Use a soft cloth. . . .") Similarly, statements of fact, such as:

*Operation* of the card reader is as follows:

when intended as instructions, should be made imperatives:

*Operate* the card reader as follows:

Note that the imperative verb is at the beginning of the imperative sentences.

## REWRITE AS IMPERATIVES

| | |
|---|---|
| Use vacuum deposition. | Vacuum deposition *must be used.* |
| | Use |

COMMENT: IN REVIEWING THESE SENTENCES NOTE THE IMMEDIACY OF THE IMPERATIVE IN CONTRAST WITH THE ROUND-ABOUT ORIGINAL.

| | |
|---|---|
| Give consideration to (Consider) alternatives. | Consideration *should be given* to alternatives. <br> Give ✓ |
| Note that the listed weights exceed. . . . | *It should be noted* that the listed weights exceed those in the specifications. |
| Check continuity with the. . . . | Continuity *is checked* with the wire-connection list and the cabling diagram. <br><br> Check |
| Remove the module by loosening the. . . . (To remove the module, loosen. . . .) | The module *is removed* by loosening the hold-down screws and pulling the module from the enclosure. |
| Align the logic chassis and the. . . . | The logic chassis and the tube chassis *are aligned* as a unit. |
| For secure connections, use the smallest holes. | For secure connections the smallest holes *should be used.* <br><br> For secure connections, |
| Adjust the power level by varying the beam voltage. | The power level *can be adjusted* by varying the beam voltage. |
| Exercise extreme caution. Be extremely cautious (careful). | Extreme caution should be exercised. |

COMMENT: MAKE WARNINGS AND CAUTIONS LIKE THE ONE IN THE PRECEDING FRAME DIRECTLY TO THE POINT. RATHER THAN WORDY EPISTLES LIKE:

WARNING: Upon application of power, voltages dangerous to life exist within this assembly. Failure to observe the necessary precautions may result in death or severe burns to personnel.

GET IT OUT IMMEDIATELY:

DANGER: Voltages in this assembly can kill.

OR JUST:

WARNING: Dangerous voltages.

INSTEAD OF A ROUNDABOUT:

If odor of gas is present, put on gas mask before entering building.

BE CONCRETE:

If *you smell* gas, put on *your* gas mask before entering the building.

## 13-2  Being Impersonal

In the first part of this chapter we recommended personal pronouns and names because of their directness and accuracy and because attempts to avoid them lead to strained, roundabout phrasing and heavy reliance on passive voice. But, though personal forms are proper (unless your organization or publication frowns on them), you should use them only when they aid in getting your message across. Do not force them into your writing in a strained attempt to be personal.

### Statements of Fact instead of Personal Observations

Remarks about feelings and beliefs should be brought out explicitly when they are central: "Our engineers *feel* that. . . ." and in conflicts of views: "Their engineers *believe* that . . . , but ours *believe* that. . . ." In other situations, make objective statements. Shun subjective ones, such as those about beliefs and feelings.

Often you can change personal observations to statements of fact by a mere deletion:

"It is felt that such devices are needlessly complex."
"Our engineers feel that their tied columns are too weak."

What remains is a simple statement of fact.

The following sentences too, make observations about facts usually at the beginning of the sentence. Delete the observation element so that you leave just the statement of fact.

### DELETE THE OBSERVATION PART OF THE STATEMENT

| | |
|---|---|
| You should note that | You should note that logic changes do not occur until the cycle ends. |
| Our staff plans that | Our staff plans that Mr. Smith will be the key investigator for the proposed program. |

COMMENT: WHEN REVIEWING THESE SENTENCES, CONCENTRATE ON THE CHANGE IN POINT OF VIEW – FROM PERSONAL TO FACTUAL.

| | |
|---|---|
| We believe that | We believe that these components will be available in June. |
| Our inspectors feel that | Our inspectors feel that the number of undetected doubles is excessive. |

| | |
|---|---|
| (It has been observed that) | It has been observed that sometimes a higher current is drawn. |
| (It is known that) | It is known that the barrier height for copper can be very low. |

### Removing "One"

Statements that rely on "one" are about as impersonally personal as English can get. For a more personal tone, you can usually change "one" to "we" or "you":

**One (We, You) can either reduce M or increase P.**

For an impersonal statement, you can sometimes delete the "one" expression:

**(One can) either reduce M or increase P.**

This sentence is still personal: "you" is understood: "[You] Either reduce. . . ." But in the following sentences, removing "one" develops impersonal statements.

*MAKE IMPERSONAL BY DELETING THE "ONE" EXPRESSION*

| | |
|---|---|
| (if one is) | More than efficiency is needed if one is to extend frequency response. |
| (one) | This integration gives one the following formula. |
| (one can expect) | Figure 6 shows the video data one can expect from a typical target. |

COMMENT: SOME SENTENCES NEED EXTENSIVE REWRITING TO REDUCE THEIR PERSONAL TONE. FOR EXAMPLE, TO REMOVE "ONE" FROM SENTENCES LIKE:

*One* must be able to produce predictable, repeatable electric properties in these devices.

YOU HAVE TO WRITE SOMETHING LIKE:

The electric properties of these devices must be predictable and repeatable" or "These devices need. . . .

### Removing Verbs Suggestive of Human Activity

In the following sentence, "made" hints at human activity:

Recent improvements *made* in this vocoder have resulted in word-intelligibility rates of. . . .

In sales proposals or requests for company support of research, it might be important to note who made the improvements—"made by our engineers" or "made by our competitors."

But the failure to mention the actor shows what is often true—that this is merely deadwood, a phony attempt to turn an impersonal message into a personal one. Impersonal statements can be developed by deleting these verbs when they are unnecessary.

Recent improvements (made) in this vocoder have resulted in. . . .

## DELETE UNNECESSARY PERSONAL VERBS

| | |
|---|---|
| (done) | Experiments done during this reporting period were more definitive. |
| (performed) | The work performed on this project included site preparation, installation, checkout, and demonstration. |
| (detected) | Immediately report improvements or delays detected. |
| (stated) | These weights exceed those stated in the specifications. |
| (used) | The substrates used were ordinary glass slides. |

By removing pseudohuman verbs from the following sentences, you will be developing another verb—an impersonal one—in its place.

Thin gold films (are found to) conduct differently.

Unlike "are found," "conduct" does not imply human activity. Sometimes the new, neutral verb will have to be rewritten slightly, as in:

The structure (was found to depend) (depended) on the temperature of the substrate.

This revision is like that in developing dynamic verbs.

## MAKE IMPERSONAL BY DELETING A VERB

| | |
|---|---|
| (made) (new verb: "will be") | The viewing hood *will be made* collapsible. (Not "will collapse") |
| increases (tends to increase) | Negative local action *tends to increase* as the battery ages. |

| | |
|---|---|
| (provided) (or: will be easy to install) | The modification kit *will be provided* in a form that is easy to install. |
| (placed) | All the equipment will be placed in one van. |
| (thought to be) (or: respond fully) | The technical details are thought to be fully responsive to the bid request. |
| responded <br> (seemed to respond) | The animal *seemed to respond* with a more feverish activity. |
| occurred <br> (was found to occur) | Complete solid-solution formation *was found to occur* in all six systems. |

COMMENT: LIMIT WORDS LIKE "SEEMS" AND "TENDS" TO THEIR PROPER SUBJECTIVE USES — TO GIVE, FOR EXAMPLE, LISTENERS' REPORTS OF DIFFERENCES IN SOUND. BUT THEN HAVE THE STATEMENT NOTE THE SUBJECTIVE NATURE OF THE EVALUATION, NOT JUST, "THE NEW SPEAKER SEEMS TO. . . ." BUT *"ACCORDING TO LISTENERS* THE NEW SPEAKER SEEMS TO. . . ." FURTHER, MAKE THESE OBSERVATIONS AS OBJECTIVE AS POSSIBLE: IF YOU CAN, SPECIFY HOW MANY LISTENERS REPORTED ONE WAY AND HOW MANY REPORTED OTHERWISE.

A statement of purpose or of intention is relevant in developing contrasts, such as:

**The address reader** *was designed to recognize* **printed addresses; it also happens to read typewritten ones.**

These allusions are often unnecessary and pseudopersonal and can raise a dangerous question: "It was designed to do that, but does it?" Such open statements can seriously undercut sales proposals and advertisements.

Remove intent and similar expressions from the following problem sentences; for example:

**The address reader was designed to recognize (recognizes). . . .**

## REWRITE IMPERSONALLY

| | |
|---|---|
| fits <br> (is designed to fit) | The interconnecting cabling *is designed to fit* under a false floor. |
| prevents <br> (is intended to prevent) | The first circuit *is intended to prevent* double transfers between the R units. |
| is (defined as) | "Real time" *is defined as* the time during which physical operations can be influenced. |
| is expanded. <br> (is chosen for expansion) | The arcing appears when the lower half of the screen is chosen for expansion. |

| | |
|---|---|
| ~~(were selected to)~~ provide (or: are) | The checks and tests in this handbook were selected to provide an effective preventive-maintenance program. |
| increases<br>~~(is directed toward increasing)~~ | The processing is directed toward increasing catalytic activity on the surface of the nickel oxide. |

**Removing "The Purpose Of" and "The Function Of"**

Remove unnecessary expressions of purpose similarly:

~~(The purpose of)~~ this test is to develop criteria for the final design.

becomes:

~~(The purpose of)~~ This test ~~(is to develop)~~ develops criteria. . . .

## REWRITE WITHOUT WORDS LIKE "FUNCTION" AND "PURPOSE"

| | |
|---|---|
| ~~(The purpose of)~~ This glossary explains ~~(is to explain)~~ the | *The purpose of* this glossary *is to explain* the terms most commonly used in the computer field. |
| Primarily<br>~~(The primary purpose of)~~ the switching panel ~~(is to prevent)~~ prevents | *The primary purpose of* the switching panel *is to prevent* either channel from attempting a third switch.<br>Primarily, the |
| ~~(The function of)~~ The editor cleans up ~~(is to clean up)~~ the | The function of the editor is to clean up the manuscript. |
| ~~(The goal of)~~ A good grounding system ~~(is to maintain)~~ maintains . . .<br>protects . . .<br>~~(to protect)~~ . . and<br>safeguards. . . .<br>. . . ~~(to safeguard)~~ | *The goal of* a good grounding system *is to maintain* continuous service, *to protect* equipment, and *to safeguard* operators. |
| ~~(It is the function of)~~ The fault register ~~(to indicate)~~ indicates | *It is the function of* the fault register *to indicate* the type of error. |
| ~~(The objective of)~~ The proposed program will ~~(be to)~~ establish | *The objective of* the proposed program *will be to establish* acoustic parameters for a speech-recognition system. |

The following sentences contain expressions like the two preceding types—"is designed" and "function."

## REWRITE IMPERSONALLY

| | |
|---|---|
| operates<br>(is designed to operate) | The campondor *is designed to operate* on a four-wire basis on the line side and on either a two- or a four-wire basis on the drop side. |
| The Pramble frames the recognition system. . . . | *The function of* the Pramble *is to frame* the recognition system with the start generator. |
| improved<br>(was installed to improve) heat transfer<br>reduced<br>and (to reduce) | A fan was installed to improve heat transfer and to reduce the skin temperature of the pump. (Two new verbs) |
| The input-output processor controls communications. | The purpose of the input-output processor is to control communications. |
| is (defined as) | A power amplifier is defined as an amplifier that delivers high power, as opposed to high voltage or high current. |
| (The function of) The mode selector and the . . . (is to) provide means for increasing (increase). . . . | The function of the mode selector and the one-bit storage register is to provide means for increasing transient response. |

## 13-3 Review

Make the following sentences more personal:

## REWRITE WITH SUGGESTED SUBJECTS

| | |
|---|---|
| Our employees will complete the drafting of the. . . . | The drafting of the circuit board *will be completed.*<br><br>Our employees ↓ |
| We assume that the error angle. . . . | It is assumed that the error angle represents the zero phase.<br><br>We |
| Their department is now designing a. . . . | A six-letter-per-second drum inserter is now being designed.<br><br>Their department is now |

| | |
|---|---|
| The authors recommend that you | It is recommended that you install another high-current distribution panel. |
| | The authors _____ (Keep the tense present.) |

Remember that imperative sentences usually start with verbs; the subject, "you," is understood: "[You] Halt."

## REWRITE AS IMPERATIVES

| | |
|---|---|
| Replace both chassis if trouble appears. | Both chassis *are replaced* if trouble appears. <br> _____ both chassis if. . . . |
| Align the undervoltage protection circuits whenever. . . . | The undervoltage-protection circuits *are aligned* whenever a module in the protection circuit is repaired or replaced. |

In becoming imperatives at least one word of the following sentences becomes superfluous, usually words like "must" or "should."

| | |
|---|---|
| Exercise care (Be careful) in. . . . | Care *must be exercised* in performing these tests. |
| Note that this system. . . . | *It should be noted* that this system refines the raw parameters by preprocessing and normalizing. |
| Keep in mind that the. . . . | *A point to* keep in mind *is* that the phase shift does not of itself distort the output. |
| Recall that, ordinarily, the D₂ line. . . . | It will be recalled that ordinarily the $D_2$ line is not recommended for optical pumping of cesium. |
| Check security daily. | Security must be checked daily. |
| Note that logic changes do not occur. . . . | It should be noted that logic changes do not occur until the cycle ends. |
| Eliminate this situation. | This situation must be eliminated. |
| However, remember that these. . . . | However, it must be remembered that these were calculated by hand. <br> However, |

Though you could turn some of the following sentences into imperatives or other personal forms, do not do so. Instead, remove their personal elements, to make them impersonal statements of fact.

## DELETE PERSONAL ELEMENTS

| | |
|---|---|
| (Experience has shown that)✔ | *Experience has shown that* either method of defining lines needs the same amount of hardware. |
| (It should be noted that)✔ | *It should be noted that* the numeric drum storage has a code number. |
| (It will be seen that)✔ | It will be seen that the clock pulse combines with nonclock time-data elements. |
| (A study of)✔ | A study of the data shows where the uncertainties occur. |
| (It has been learned that)✔ | It has been learned that the indications given by this alarm are not reliable. |
| (It is known that)✔ | It is known that heat increases resistance. |
| (It is felt that)✔ | It is felt that a simple design will save money. |
| (made)✔ (Rubber pads) | Pads made of rubber isolate the frame from the case. |
| (was added)✔ . . . ,(which)✔ | A second modification *was added* to the motor, *which* increased reliability. |

COMMENT: THE GRATUITOUS PERSONAL "IF MET" IN THE FOLLOWING SENTENCE ACTUALLY CHALLENGES THE SALES OFFER:

These specifications will, *if met,* ensure that we are satisfying all your requirements.

THIS SUGGESTS THAT THE SPECIFICATION MIGHT NOT BE MET:

We will do what you require, but then, too, we might not.

To make the following sentences impersonal, you will have to develop new verbs.

## REWRITE IMPERSONALLY

| | |
|---|---|
| recognizes (is designed to recognize)✔ | The character reader *is designed to recognize* characters in two steps. |

| | |
|---|---|
| contained<br>(were found to contain) | The valves *were found to contain* metal chips. (Keep the tense past.) |
| reduces<br>(offers a reduction in) | This circuit offers a reduction in the hardware in the comparison network. |
| (The objective of) This manual reports<br>(is to report) on | *The objective of* this manual *is to report on* printed-circuit information we gathered during the past year. |
| (The function of) The program section interprets executes (is to interpret) and (to execute) | The function of the program section is to interpret and execute instructions. |
| depend (depended)<br>(were observed to depend) | Their properties were observed to depend on the rate of deposition. |
| dislodges<br>(tends to dislodge) | Gassing tends to dislodge active material from the battery plates. |
| improved slightly<br>(showed a slight improvement) | The condition showed a slight improvement.<br><br>((Use "slightly")) |
| (Inspection of) Equations 5 and 7 show<br>(shows) that | *Inspection of* equations 5 and 7 *shows* that we yet have to find the variables.<br>Equations 5 and 7 |
| (The purpose of) This equipment accepts, analyzes, and reports (is to accept, analyze, and report) | The purpose of this equipment is to accept, analyze, and report system failures. (Three verbs) |
| are (provided as) | Handles are provided as a part of the Klystron assembly. |
| crystallizes<br>(is known to crystallize) | Gallium arsenide is known to crystallize only in the cubic zinc blende structure. |
| (tend to) increase | Since welded joints tend to increase the cost, we soldered all joints. |
| (seem to) occur | As the graph shows, permanent changes *seem to occur* only gradually. |
| increases<br>(offers increased) | The new method offers increased performance. |
| is (defined as) | A space charge is defined as a charge of electricity distributed throughout a three-dimensional medium. |

| | |
|---|---|
| delivers<br>~~is designed to deliver~~ | The blower is designed to deliver approximately 500 cubic feet per minute against a pressure of 2 inches of water. |
| ~~The purpose of~~ Prestart cycling<br>warms<br>~~is to warm~~ | The purpose of prestart cycling is to warm the tubes before the full load is applied. |
| will ~~be designed to~~ match | Lines from the memory stack will be designed to match the characteristic impedance of the stack, thereby minimizing reflections. |
| describes<br>~~In~~ This paper ~~we describe~~ | In this paper we describe methods of depositing films. |
| Transmission increased as much as 50 percent. | Increases in transmission of as much as 50 percent could be observed. |

COMMENT: YOU CAN BYPASS MUCH PSEUDOPERSONALIZING BY REPLACING VERBS THAT HINT AT HUMAN ACTIVITY WITH NEUTRAL ONES. RATHER THAN:

An absorption cell *was placed* in front of the laser.

IN WHICH "WAS PLACED" LOOKS TO SOMEONE WHO DID THE PLACING, YOU CAN STRESS EITHER THE CELL:

An absorption cell *stood* in front of the laser.

OR YOU CAN STRESS THE LASER:

The laser *faced* an absorption cell.

NEITHER SENTENCE IMPLIES HUMAN ACTIVITY: THE CELL STANDS; THE LASER FACES.

# PUNCTUATION

Punctuation is a highly complex study. Most technical writers avoid its complications by punctuating as little as possible. This is in tune with the modern approach to punctuation. Accordingly, this chapter concentrates on the marks most frequently misused in technical writing: hyphens in unit modifiers and commas.

## 14-1 Periods, Semicolons, and Colons

Technical writers, for the most part, shun variety in end (terminal) punctuation simply by ending most sentences with periods. If you want to, you can add a bit of variety at times by using semicolons and colons instead of periods. Put semicolons between independent clauses (clauses that can stand by themselves as sentences) if the clauses are closely related in thought:

Connect a jumper wire from J1 to J2; if the bulb lights, press push-button indicator PB-4.

Put a colon between independent clauses when the first introduces the second:

Clipping the large amplitude can be tolerated: little information is present at that level.

Related uses of the colon are in salutations of business letters ("Dear Mr. James:") and in introducing listings ("We suggest the following: A . . . , B . . . ," etc.). But periods can almost always replace semicolons and colons as end punctuation marks.

## 14-2   Commas: In Series and between Independent Clauses

Many writers do have trouble with commas. They usually know that they should use them between items in a series:

**We need only a rack, the three modules, the digital generator, and the voltmeter.**

The comma with the "and" preceding the last item in the above series is customary in technical writing; it is often omitted in other writing. When only two items are joined by connectives, do not use commas:

**They shipped the tachometer and the dwell meter.**

Most writers also know that they should use commas between independent clauses joined by the coordinating conjuctions: "and," "but," "or," "nor," and "yet."

**No signal power is lost, and the sharp degradation of an ordinary binary system disappears.**

**He overhauled the transmission, but it still slips.**

This combination of a comma and a conjunction between independent clauses acts very much like periods, semicolons, and colons between them. Periods, however, signal the strongest stop, semicolons less than that, the combination of comma and conjunction least of all. The colon, of course, is used when the first element introduces the second.

### INSERT COMMAS IN SERIES AND BETWEEN INDEPENDENT CLAUSES

| | |
|---|---|
| differences; and (differences; these) | We noted the numbers of the positions where there are *r* differences and these are given below. (Independent clauses) |
| thin-film; | This is a report on thin-film metal-base transistors. (Use one comma.) |
| averages; and (averages; inexperienced) | Experienced listeners consistently had higher averages and inexperienced listeners consistently had lower averages. |
| deflection, strain, temperature, and. . . . | This symposium also gives the analysis of deflection strain temperature and other measurements on several Italian dams. (Three commas) |
| period, but (period; the laser) | We tried to finish the experiment during the last report period but the laser had been damaged in transit. |

| secondary, | Fortify the basic system with secondary permanent installations. (Two adjectives describing the installations) |
|---|---|
| problems, and (problems; lasing) | We are taking steps to eliminate these problems and lasing with the rotating prism is expected soon. |
| used, and (used; 1-kilowatt) | Dual diversity is used and 1-kilowatt power amplifiers are needed. |
| the equipment, voltages, and current. | This section lists the equipment voltages and current. (two commas) |

## 14-3  Commas with Interpolated Material

An important use of the comma is in enclosing interpolated material that is not essential. For example, the appositive in the following sentence is not essential:

**The power supply cabinet,** *a 1-in-1 cabinet,* **houses the power supplies and the control panels.**

You can see this is not essential material because the meaning of the sentence does not change when it is omitted. It is added information.

### Essential and Nonessential Material

Now read the following sentence with and without the italicized material. Is it essential? Or is it nonessential, in which case it should be set off in commas?

**Water** *which is composed of hydrogen and oxygen* **can be broken down chemically.**

It is supplementary, not necessary to the meaning of the sentence, namely, that water can be broken down chemically. It should be set off by commas to show that it is supplementary. Is the italicized expression in the following sentence necessary to its meaning? Or should it be between commas?

**Water** *that has been boiled ten minutes* **is safe to drink.**

This is essential material. Without it the sentence changes in meaning. The message is not: "Water is safe to drink." Do not enclose this kind of essential material in commas.

If the material interpolated in the following sentences is not essential, insert commas.

## CIRCLE "ESSENTIAL" OR "NOT ESSENTIAL." INSERT COMMAS IF NOT ESSENTIAL

| | |
|---|---|
| Essential (no commas) | Activities of our company *that are directly related to this program* are performed by the Electronics Communications Division. (If the italicized material can be deleted, it is not essential: Are all activities performed by that one division?) <br><br> Essential/Not essential (Insert commas) |
| Not essential (limitations , ) | Chemical and structural considerations, however, impose other limitations *with the result that Ag is the most likely substitute.* <br><br> Essential/Not essential (Is this added information?) |
| Depends on the meaning intended. With a comma this is just added information about the amplifiers. Without the comma, the circuit controls only those amplifiers whose outputs vary more than 50 decibels, and no others. | This circuit controls the gain of the amplifiers *whose outputs vary more than 50 decibels.* <br><br> Essential/Not essential (Insert commas.) <br><br> (Note how a comma changes the meaning.) |
| Essential <br><br> (Commas would mean that all technicians are new to the equipment.) | Technicians *who are new to this equipment* should not attempt any adjustments or alignments. <br><br> Essential/Not essential |
| Not essential <br><br> (increases , ) <br><br> (supplementary information) | The emitter impedance increases *which further reduces the gain.* <br><br> Essential/Not essential |
| Not essential <br><br> , if one is available , | This information is sent to an outgoing line *if one is available* or to intermediate storage. (Added information: when it is sent.) <br><br> Essential/Not essential |
| Depends on the meaning intended. Some writers use "which" to indicate nonessential material; "that," essential. | The graduate *which both used* is missing. <br><br> Essential/Not essential |

| | |
|---|---|
| With a comma, this is just supplementary information about the only valve. Without a comma, this discusses one valve, ignoring similar ones not near the amplifier. | An important feature is the thermodivert valve which is near the amplifier. |
| | Essential/Not essential |
| | (Note how a comma changes the meaning.) |
| Essential | Do you recall *when it started?* |
| | Essential/Not essential |
| Not essential | We examined these films by reflection electron diffraction on the 110 azimuth *where twinning can most easily be detected.* |
| (azimuth , ) | |
| | Essential/Not essential |

### In the Body of the Sentence

The interpolated material in the following sentences is nonessential. Since it is in the body of the sentence — not at its beginning or end — it should be enclosed between two commas.

*ENCLOSE INTERPOLATED MATERIAL IN COMMAS*

| | |
|---|---|
| , which generally . . . in a PABX , | Dial pulsing which generally occurs on calls terminating in a PABX has ten pulses a second. |
| , an integrator module , | Module 14 an integrator module energizes next. |
| , B. | The formula below gives the probability B. ("B" is the symbol for probability.) |
| , because of its . . . capacity , | Our monitor because of its greater input-output capacity is more flexible. |

### At the Beginning of the Sentence

The interpolated, nonessential material is at the beginning of the following sentences. It includes transitional words, such as "however," "therefore," "nevertheless," "moreover," and "furthermore."

*However,* we have not begun to work on that phase of the project.

(You can usually replace such weighty connectives with lighterweight ones.) Most of the following sentences need commas for clarity. The reason for others is given at the left with the correct punctuation. Insert one comma between the introductory expressions and the rest of the sentence.

| | |
|---|---|
| observed ; <br><br> (Introductory dependent clause) | As our chemists observed the change is too rapid. |
| loss ; <br><br> (For clarity) | Because of the partial loss higher concentrations might appear in the film compounds. |
| Essentially ; | Essentially module 7 is a frequency generator. |
| error, <br><br> (Introductory dependent clause. These are always followed by a comma.) | When the program detects an error it prints the error code and stops. |
| turn-on, | At power turn-on module 5 energizes. |
| filtering, | After filtering the dc control current activates the second stage. |
| past, | As in the past strips of gold film were deposited on another film. |
| processing, | With data processing the speed will about triple. |

### At the End of the Sentence

The interpolated material is at the end of the following problem sentences. Insert a comma to separate it from the rest of the sentence.

*SET OFF THE INTERPOLATED MATERIAL AT THE END OF THE SENTENCE*

| | |
|---|---|
| main clock pulse ; | The complementary clock pulse is delayed in relation to the main clock pulse thus activating the combinational logic circuit. |
| two subsignals ; <br> ("And" merely connects two elements: "one for the . . . and one for the. . . .") | This signal separates into two subsignals one for the baseband and one for the spectrum channels. (No comma needed before "and") |
| characteristic ; | It has an excellent forward-resistance characteristic with a forward resistance of 0.2. |

| | |
|---|---|
| each, | The total length is 128 words of 32 bits each or 4,096 bits. |
| axis, | The darker image at the left was produced by light polarized parallel to the C axis for which light the absorption edge is deeper in the red end of the spectrum than the absorption edge for light polarized perpendicular to the C axis. |

### Comma Review

The interpolated expression may be anywhere in the following sentences. When it is in the body of the sentence, set it between two commas.

| | |
|---|---|
| block; | Up to twenty-four channel links can use this frequency block while up to sixty can use the other. ("While" acts like "but.") |
| devices (;)<br><br>(Reread, noting how a comma changes the meaning.) | This heat must be removed by special devices which further add to the cost, weight, and inefficiency. |
| 7 to 14;<br><br>(A dependent clause introducing an independent one) | If we let $n$ have values from 7 to 14 we can calculate the positions that have $n$ differences. |
| , which has a high . . . impedance, | This amplifier which has a high input impedance will not do. |
| power, | Flashtubes operate at extremely high power which they can sustain for short periods of time only. |
| four, | The zinc blende structure is restricted to compositions that have an average valence of four which on the tetrahedral representation are in the square containing III-IV compounds. |
| , which we . . . analysis, | The lattice parameters of these crystals which we found by x-ray analysis agree with the values given by Dönges. |
| data,<br><br>(Introductory dependent clause) | Since Figure 1 shows this data you can use it as your guide. |

| | |
|---|---|
| channels, | Their study showed that time multiplexing can reduce the number of channels the amount of time sharing depending on the radar parameters. |
| , or air line, | The air gap *or air line* is the distance between the armature and the heel piece *when the relay is energized.* (Must both be set off by commas, or is the second necessary?) |
| valve, (Introductory dependent clause) | If you plan to open the safety valve turn off the burner. |
| 30, (For clarity) | Make changes by way of stages 19 through 30 and 42 through 50. |

## 14-4  Hyphening Unit Modifiers in Phrases

The hyphenation of compound words is complex and everchanging. The *United States Government Printing Office Style Manual* devotes many pages to it. The following concentrates on a common weakness in technical writing, the hyphening of unit modifiers.

Modifiers are words that change the meaning of other words: "card" in "a card deck" modifies "deck," limiting consideration to that kind of deck and excluding "mail decks" and "yacht decks." A modifier of more than one word when it precedes the word being modified should be hyphened: "a mixed-mail deck." Usually when the two-word modifier follows the word it modifies, it is not hyphened: "A well-advanced study," but "This study is well advanced."

The hyphen shows that the two words act together, as unit modifiers. Without the hyphens readers have difficulty distinguishing modifiers from words being modified. This difficulty increases geometrically when there is more than one modifier ("the azimuth angle, servo data correction signal") and when the unit modifier consists of more than two words ("the pedestal power disconnect contact relay").

### Two-word Unit Modifiers

Unit modifiers in the following frames are of two words and precede the word modified, as in "mixed-mail deck." When reviewing these sentences, note how the hyphens clarify the relation between modifiers and modified.

## HYPHEN THE TWO-WORD MODIFIER

| | |
|---|---|
| the zero crossing indicator | the zero crossing indicator |

(The arrow points to the word being modified.)

| | |
|---|---|
| the near limit switches | the near limit switches |
| a 200 kilocycle signal | a 200 kilocycle signal |
| for clipped baseband speech | for clipped baseband speech |

In the following frames both the modifier and the word to be modified are of
two words, as in:

**the data servo error signal**

which means:

**the data-servo** error signal.

## HYPHEN THE MODIFIER

| | |
|---|---|
| an all electronic character reader | an all electronic character reader |
| a 10 bit shift register | a 10 bit shift register |
| a low pass smoothing filter | a low pass smoothing filter |
| a time-domain pitch extractor | a time domain pitch extractor |

### Three-word Unit Modifiers

The unit modifiers in the following frames consist of three words, as in "the
card-to-tape operation."

## HYPHEN THREE-WORD MODIFIERS

| | |
|---|---|
| the carrier to noise ratio | the carrier to noise ratio |
| a tape to card conversion | a tape to card conversion |

| | |
|---|---|
| these sample-and-hold circuits | these sample and hold circuits |
| the card-to-tape operation | the card to tape operation |

COMMENT: HYPHENING HELPS PREVENT AMBIGUITY. FOR EXAMPLE, THE UNHYPHENED:

The three color status boards.

MAY MEAN THREE BOARDS:

The *three* color-status boards (Three boards showing the status *of* colors)

OR THREE COLORS:

The *three-color* status boards (The boards showing the status *by using* three colors)

HYPHENING HELPS MAKE CLEAR THE INTENDED RELATIONSHIP.


### Two Unit Modifiers

Sometimes two unit modifiers work together, as in:

Thin-film, metal-base transistors

Sometimes, part of one unit modifier is missing, that is, understood, as in:

A two- or three-level process.

which means:

A two-level or three-level process.

It is usually better to follow the second example: write out both modifiers.

## HYPHEN BOTH MODIFIERS

| | |
|---|---|
| 50-cycle, high-pass filter | 50 cycle, high pass filter |
| azimuth-angle, servo-data correction | azimuth angle, servo data correction |
| half- to full-wave rectification | half to full wave rectification (i.e., half wave to full wave rectification) |
| A constant-level, speech-processing system | A constant level, speech processing system |

| The azimuth-circuit, search-channel conversion | The azimuth circuit, search channel conversion |

### Hyphen Review

The following frames contain a mixture of the preceding types of unit modifiers:

*HYPHEN MODIFIERS*

| our hand-print reader | our hand print reader |
| its word-identity and card-location code | its word identity and card location code |
| a 1-kilowatt power amplifier | a 1 kilowatt power amplifier |
| for thin-film, metal-base transistors | for thin film, metal base transistors |
| the yoke-driver amplifier | the yoke driver amplifier |

## 14-5  Hyphening Unit Modifiers in Sentences

The unit modifiers are in sentences in the following frames.

### Two-word Unit Modifiers

*HYPHEN TWO-WORD MODIFIERS*

| Count from the ten-mile pip. | Count from the ten mile pip. |
| We installed a time-delay relay. | We installed a time delay relay. |
| This is a five-man team. | This is a five man team. |
| For low-energy carriers this factor is . . . | For low energy carriers this factor is important only at low temperatures. |

### Three-word Unit Modifiers

*HYPHEN THREE-WORD MODIFIERS*

| All class-of-service information. . . . | All *class of service* information shifts at that time. |

| | |
|---|---|
| . . . the rate-of-change adjustment. | The waveform responds only to the rate of change adjustment. |
| . . . a change-of-state technique. | Use a change of state technique. |
| A high signal-to-noise ratio indicates. . . . | A high signal to noise ratio indicates peak performance. |
| . . . we used analog-to-digital converters. | On this program we used analog to digital converters. |

COMMENT: THE FOLLOWING ARE IMPORTANT EXCEPTIONS TO THE GENERAL RULE TO HYPHEN ALL UNIT MODIFIERS.
1. DON'T HYPHEN PROPER NOUNS:

The George Morris Company

2. DON'T HYPHEN CHEMICAL COMPOUNDS:

NaCl; zinc sulfide

3. DON'T HYPHEN TWO WORDS WHEN THE FIRST ENDS IN "-LY." WORDS ENDING IN "-LY" ARE USUALLY ADVERBS, WHICH SELDOM CAN BE TAKEN TO MODIFY NOUNS:

"A highly touted drug"; "highly" modifies "touted."

4. DON'T HYPHEN A NOUN FOLLOWED BY A NUMBER OR A LETTER, AS IN

"Type A substance," "channel 1 conversion."

5. DON'T HYPHEN EXPRESSIONS THAT ARE SO COMMON THERE IS LITTLE CHANCE OF MISUNDERSTANDING, FOR EXAMPLE,

"Cathode ray tube."

> BUT BE CAREFUL WHAT YOU TAKE TO BE COMMON USE. OFTEN, THE COMMON USAGE IN ONE DEPARTMENT OR LABORATORY IS NOT EVEN KNOWN IN OTHER DEPARTMENTS OF THE SAME COMPANY. USE AS YOUR CRITERION THE USAGES OF PUBLICATIONS IN YOUR FIELD.

## 14-6   Review

### INSERT COMMAS

| | |
|---|---|
| 208 bits, <br><br>(The expression following "and" cannot stand by itself) | Each frame consists of 208 bits 48 bits for the spectrum channels and 160 bits for the the baseband. (The comma does not go before "and.") |
| , therefore, <br><br>(The expression following "and" cannot stand by itself.) | This value ensures that $\Delta\phi$ is small and *therefore* that the preceding assumption is valid. (Comma not needed before "and.") |

| | |
|---|---|
| tests , <br><br> (Introductory dependent clause) | After the reader failed the first tests they developed less stringent tests. |
| switch, S1, | The selector switch S1 starts the motor. |
| , a . . . relay, | This relay a slow-operate relay then activates. |
| zero, <br><br> (Introductory dependent clause) | When the pointer is on zero restart the timer. |
| processor, <br><br> (Unless there is more than one final processor and this is singling out one of them.) | This information is sent to the final processor where final processing is accomplished. |
| spandrels, . . . curves, | The spandrels the spaces above the curves are decorated. |
| weight, | The extrusion increased the weight which added to the cost. |
| 1970, | When the prototype was set up in 1970 the turnstiles were automatic. |
| resistance, | Solve for the resistance R. |
| condemned, | When the field was condemned the strata was taken out of production. |
| McNichol, . . . editor, | Mr. J. McNichol a leading editor designed the type face. |
| Unfortunately, | Unfortunately the swage slipped to the left. |
| 5, | The blanks go to Station 5 where the cutters open them. |
| away, | The tang rusted away and the face filled with rust. |
| processor, . . . model, | The central processor a new model cannot handle the data. |

## HYPHEN UNIT MODIFIERS

| | |
|---|---|
| for service-request signals. | The scanner examines every terminal for service request signals. |

| | |
|---|---|
| surface-barrier transistor. | We have tested this type of interface on a surface barrier transistor. |
| step-by-step instructions | Each kit contains step by step instructions for installation. |
| the type-out cycle | Is the type out cycle complete? |
| low-level, high-frequency components. | This eliminated the discrimination against low level, high frequency components. (There are two.) |
| the high-vacuum pump | They have repaired the high vacuum pump. |
| the aperture-to-medium coupling loss. | This will increase the *aperture to medium* coupling loss. |
| The two-level signal | The circuit then samples the two level signal. |
| A direct-view tube is | A direct view tube is more convenient. |
| agreed-on time | To complete the project in the *agreed on* time, we have to take this approach. |
| The fixed-station antennas | You can easily turn the *fixed station* antennas. |
| free-carrier absorption | Wherever the beam impacted, there was free carrier absorption. |
| the audio-frequency lines | It is the central location for equipment used in testing the audio frequency lines. |
| The azimuth-direction, gate-generator signal | The azimuth direction, gate generator signal changes the current in the coil. (There are two.) |
| on a four-wire basis . . . and on a two- or four-wire basis | The campondor operates on a four wire basis on the line side and on a two or a four wire basis on the drop side. (There are three.) |

# EMPHASIZING AND SUBORDINATING

Diffuse sentences stifle verb impact, sometimes because the sentences are overly long, sometimes because they fail to give precedence to important ideas.

## 15-1  Breaking Up Long Sentences

Long sentences strain both your competence and your reader's comprehension. So generally keep sentences short. We earlier shortened sentences simply by taking words out of them. Sometimes, however, we have to break them into two or more. In fact, if you find yourself struggling to clarify a sentence or if one seems involved, try dividing its ideas between two or more sentences. This will often bypass the difficulty completely.

### New Subject in the Second Clause

Most of the following sentences contain "and," "that," or "which." Break them into two sentences at that word. Insert a period where the first sentence ends. Then rewrite the remainder; use as its subject a word already in the sentence. If you run into difficulties, check upper left, which shows where the first sentence ends.

---

*INSERT A PERIOD. THEN MAKE A SENTENCE OF THE REMAINDER*

---

. . . generates the data. and . . .

. . . generates the data. This pulse delays. . . .

The complement of the clock pulse generates the data, *and* this pulse delays in relation to the clock pulse that activates the combining logic.

189

| | |
|---|---|
| . . . onto punch cards. (and) these . . . | The CBU transfers the machine-language program onto punch cards, *and* these cards form the program deck. |
| . . . onto punch cards. These cards form the program deck. | |

### New Subject: "It"

Use "it" as the subject of the following sentences.

| | |
|---|---|
| . . . to 0.003 in. (and) is regulated . . . | The clearance should be 0.002 to 0.003 inch *and* is regulated by the armature-adjusting screw. |
| . . . to 0.003 inch. It is regulated by. . . . | |
| . . . a 1-in-1 cabinet. (that) houses the . . . | The power-supply cabinet is a 1-in-1 cabinet *that* houses the power supplies and the control panels for the automatic monitoring circuits. |
| . . . a 1-in-1 cabinet. It houses the . . . | |
| . . . adaptable system. (that) conforms to the . . . | This is a flexible and adaptable system *that* conforms to the specification and performs well. |
| . . . adaptable system. It conforms to the . . . | |

### "This" or "These" as Part of the New Subject

Use "this" or "these" in the following sentences to form *part only* of the subject for the second sentence.

| | |
|---|---|
| . . . events combine. from (which) information. . . . | The computer analyzes the information and tabulates it according to how often the events combine, from *which* information we choose the best levels. (Use "from this information.") |
| . . . events combine. From this information we choose . . . | |
| . . . Air Command. all (of which) stations . . . | As of June 1968 our company had completed several stations of an automatically controlled HF SSB and UHF radio system for the Air Command, *all of which* stations the government has accepted. |
| . . . Air Command. All these stations the government . . . (or: The government has) | |
| channel. one of (which) will be . . . | Each frame contains 208 bits, 160 for the baseband and 48 for the spectrum channel, *one of which* we use for framing. (Use "these bits.") |
| channel. One of these bits we | |

| | |
|---|---|
| . . . sorting processes. (by using) ✓ the . . . <br> . . . sorting processes. You can use the author sort. . . . | If you sort author names first, you can take advantage of operations common to both sorting processes *by using* the author sort as input to the subject sort. (Use "You can.") |
| . . . frame. (which) . . . compo-nents. and which also. . . . <br> . . . frame. This frame is a. . . . components. It also connects. . . . | Structural stability comes from a cast-aluminum "figure-eight" frame, *which* is a base for mounting other components *and which* also connects the set to a portable electronic tester. (Three sentences: Use "This frame" and "It.") |
| . . . aligning fields. (in the sense) ✓ (that) the . . . stray-field direction. and causing. . . . <br> . . . fields. At that value the pumped atoms . . . direction. This causes system disorientation. | The effects of stray fields appears at the zero value of the aligning fields, *in the sense that* the pumped atoms try to precess in the stray-field direction, *causing* system disorientation. (Three sentences: Use "At that value" and "This.") |

## 15-2 Subordinating with "-ing"

Though short sentences are usually desirable because of their direct, immediate impact, not all sentences should be short. Vary their length. Mix longer sentences with short ones. This will avoid the clipped monotony of short Dick-and-Jane sentences. But in any question of clarity, rely on short sentences. Always prefer short, clear sentences to varied but unclear ones.

One of the benefits of some longer sentences is that you can subordinate ideas and emphasize others, showing their relationship more exactly.

The following sentences present two ideas on the same level of importance:

**This manual** *has* **the maintenance information.**

**Information in this manual** *includes* **preventive maintenance, troubleshooting, and aligning.**

Yet the idea in the second sentence is secondary to that in the first. It can be de-emphasized by softening the impact of its verb, changing "includes" to its "-ing" form, "including":

**This manual** *has* **the maintenance information,** *including* **preventive maintenance, troubleshooting, and aligning.**

Subordinate the second of the following sentences similarly with an "-ing" form preceded (as above) by a comma. In reviewing the frames, note how the revision of the second verb softens its force.

## SUBORDINATE THE SECOND SENTENCE BY CHANGING ITS VERB TO AN "-ING" FORM

| | |
|---|---|
| . . . range, *noting* whether the meter moves. . . . | Turn potentiometer X through its entire range. *Note* whether the needle moves out of the green. |
| . . . maser system, (his work) *including* its high-vacuum systems. . . . | He supervised the mechanical design of the entire maser system. His work *included* its high-vacuum systems, cryogenics, and microwave engineering. |
| . . . system, the reason *being* its simplicity and. . . . (because of its simplicity) | We selected the single-network code system. The reason *was* its simplicity and low cost. ("Being" is the "-ing" form of "was.") |

You have already broken some of the following sentences into two sentences. Now subordinate the second part of the sentence to the first by changing its verb to an "-ing" form, being sure to delete "and."

| | |
|---|---|
| . . . controlled, (and) *being* held to less than. . . . | The evaporation rate is more rigidly controlled *and* is held to less than 1 percent. (Use "being.") |
| . . . the data, (and) this pulse *being delayed* in relation to. . . . | The complement of the clock pulse generates the data, *and* this pulse *is* delayed in relation to the clock pulse. |
| . . . onto punch cards, (and) these cards *forming* the program deck. | The CBU transfers the machine-language program onto punch cards, *and* these cards *form* the program deck. |

Subordinate the second element in the following sentences similarly with an "-ing" form:

| | |
|---|---|
| , with error rates *equaling* that of humans. | The formant locations give enough information, with error rates *equal to* that of humans. |
| . . . service, *protecting* equipment and *safeguarding* operators. | A good grounding system maintains continuous service, *protects* equipment, and *safeguards* operators. |
| . . . capacity, (and) thereby *improving* the signal-to-noise ratio. | The additional reflections doubled the light-gathering capacity *and* thereby *improved* the signal-to-noise ratio. |

## 15-3   Subordinating in Appositional or Similar Forms

You can deemphasize material in some sentences by putting it in appositional or similar forms.

### Subordinating the Idea Following the First Verb

Most of the following sentences contain two verbs. Subordinate the idea connected with and following the first verb. Do this by removing the verb and enclosing the entire expression in commas. For example:

**The temperature controller** *is near the infrared detector and* **operates like a thermistor.**

can be rewritten:

**The temperature controller,** *is near the infrared detector,* **and operates like a thermistor.**

In the following sentences similarly subordinate the thought following the first verb. Be sure you remove all unnecessary words, such as "and" in the above sentence, before checking left.

### SUBORDINATE THE THOUGHT FOLLOWING THE FIRST VERB

| | |
|---|---|
| The FM deviator , is an RC phase-shift oscillator , that produces a. . . . | The FM deviator *is an RC phase-shift oscillator* that produces a highly linear FM carrier. |
| Site preparation , is the next step , and it is very important. | Site preparation *is the next step, and* it is very important. |
| The clearance , 0.002 to 0.003 inch , is regulated by the . . . | The clearance *should be 0.002 to 0.003 inch and* is regulated by the armature-adjusting screw. |
| Mr. Rykaczewski and Mr. Scheurer , (who were) key researchers on the . . . program , will work on the proposed program. | Mr. Rykaczewski and Mr. Scheurer were key researchers on the advanced speech-recognition program and will work on the proposed program. |

COMMENT: DON'T MAKE THESE CHANGES CARELESSLY. IT WOULD NOT BE RIGHT, FOR EXAMPLE, TO CHANGE THE SENTENCE:

The power supply *is diagramed in Figure 10,* which lists all input and output voltages.

TO THE FOLLOWING:

The power supply, *diagramed in Figure 10,* lists all input and output voltages.

FIGURE 10 MIGHT LIST VOLTAGES; A POWER SUPPLY WOULD NOT.

The following sentences have an infinitive (a "to" form) in their second element. Continue subordinating the idea following the first verb. Change the infinitive to another form of verb. Since the infinitive here suggests purpose, eliminating it will make the sentence less personal. Commas are not needed.

| | |
|---|---|
| Logic (is) in the circuit (to shift) [shifts] the. . . . | Logic *is* in the circuit *to shift* the processing channel automatically. |
| A small thermostat (is) on the body . . . (to remove) the beam. [removes] . . . | A small thermostat *is* on the body of the Klystron *to remove* the beam voltage at 175°F. |
| Jack and lamp panels (are included) in the bay (to provide) for. . . . [provide] | Jack and lamp panels *are included* in the bay *to provide* for test-bay lines. |
| A designation strip (is fastened) at the top and bottom . . . (to identify) the. . . . [identifies] | A designation strip is fastened at the top and bottom of each panel to identify the circuit. |

Continue changing the infinitive in the second element to another verb form. Remove only the auxiliary from the first verb.

| | |
|---|---|
| The ten listeners (were) selected at random (to take) the test. [took] | The ten listeners *were selected* at random to *take* the test. (Delete "were.") |
| | The ten listeners _____ took the test. |
| Queries (are) programmed onto punch cards (to check) all points. . . . [check] . . . | Queries *are programmed* onto punch cards to *check* all test points sequentially. |
| A rounding-off routine (was) added to the program (to handle) fractions. [handles] | A rounding-off routine *was added* to the program *to handle* fractions. |

### Subordinating the Idea Following the Second Verb

You can similarly subordinate the thought expressed with the second verb. Just move it in front of the first verb, and put "which" before it. For example, consider the italicized material in:

**The power supply cabinet is a 1-in-1 cabinet** *that houses the power supplies and the control panel.*

This is subordinated in the following revision:

**The power supply cabinet,** *which houses the power supplies and the control panel,* **is a 1-in-1 cabinet.**

Insert all commas, and reread the sentence carefully before checking left.

## *SUBORDINATE THE IDEA EXPRESSED BY THE SECOND VERB. USE "WHICH"*

| | |
|---|---|
| Site preparation, which is very important, is the next step. | Site preparation is the next step, *and it is very important.*<br><br>Site preparation, which is very _____ is _____ . |
| The clearance, which is regulated by the . . . screw, should be. . . . | The clearance should be 0.002 to 0.003 inch *and is regulated by the armature-adjusting screw.*<br><br>The clearance, which is regulated _____, should _____ . |
| The temperature controller, which operates like a thermistor, is near the. . . . | The temperature controller is near the infrared detector *and operates like a thermistor.* |
| The synchronizer, which houses two identical timers, is an 8-in-1 cabinet. | The synchronizer is an 8-in-1 cabinet that houses two identical timers. |
| A small thermostat, which removes the beam voltage at 175°F, is on the. . . . | A small thermostat is on the body of the Klystron to remove beam voltage at 175°F. |
| The dummy load, which has circuits that sense leaks, is a. . . . | The dummy load is a resistive water wedge that has circuits that sense leaks. |
| The timer, which times intervals of up to ten hours, sends signals. . . . | The timer sends signals through the clock system and times intervals of up to ten hours. |

The second element in the following sentences has an infinitive. Subordinate the second element, using "which." Change the infinitive to another verb form. Commas are not needed.

## SUBORDINATE THE SECOND ELEMENT

| | |
|---|---|
| A rounding-off routine *which handles* fractions was added to the program. | A rounding-off routine was added to the program *to handle fractions*. |
| Jack and lamp panels (*which provide*) for test-bay lines are (included) in the bay. | Jack and lamp panels are included in the bay *to provide for test-bay lines*. |
| A diode *which reduces* ac ripple is (included) in the filter. | A diode is included in the filter *to reduce ac ripple*. |
| | A diode which |
| The ten listeners *who took* the test were selected at random. | The ten listeners were selected at random *to take the test*. |
| | The ten listeners who |
| A designation strip which identifies the circuits is (fastened) at the top . . . | A designation strip is fastened at the top and bottom of each panel to identify the circuits. |

### 15-4  Replacing Verbs with Prepositions

In the following sentences you can emphasize the second verb by replacing the first one with a preposition and transposing words around it. For example, the sentence:

The set *has* two identical panels which act as card carriers.

becomes:

Two identical panels *on* the set (which) act as card carriers.

"On" takes the place of "has." The original subject exchanges places with the new subject on the opposite side of the preposition. Revise the following sentences similarly, using the suggested preposition. Should you run into difficulty, the upper left gives the new subject.

## REPLACE THE FIRST VERB WITH PREPOSITIONS, TRANSPOSING OTHER WORDS

| | |
|---|---|
| Check valves<br>Check valves on the hoses prevent the coolant from. . . . | The hoses are fitted with check valves to prevent the coolant from draining off.<br><br>Check valves on |

Test points
Test points on the operations control board connect to circuits. . . .

The operations control board has test points that connect to circuits throughout the station. (on)

Test points *on*

---

One factor in
One factor in this machine limits its use. (One factor limits the use of this machine.)

This machine has *one factor* that limits its use.

One factor *in*

---

A transparent door on
A transparent door on the sloping part of the cabinet pivots up. . . .

The sloping part of the cabinet contains *a transparent door* that pivots up into the cabinet. (on)

A transparent door *on*

---

Sharp edges on
Sharp edges on the picker head caught unsealed flaps.

The picker head had *sharp edges* which caught unsealed flaps. (on)

---

A knob at
A knob at each position controls the light intensity.

Each position has *a knob* for controlling the light intensity. (at)

---

The two sections of
The two sections of this chapter contain. . . .

This chapter is divided into *two sections* which contain the following information. (of)

The two sections

---

Signals from
Signals from the timer synchronize the radar set.

The timer produces signals that synchronize the radar set. (from)

---

Prerecorded pulses
Prerecorded pulses on the timing tracks are used as. . . .

The timing tracks contain prerecorded pulses which are used as timing signals. (on)

---

Smoke and haze from
Smoke and haze from jungle fires prevented surveys.

Jungle fires caused smoke and haze, which prevented surveys. (from)

---

## 15-5  Review

Make two sentences of each of the following. If you run into difficulties, the upper left shows where to insert the first period. Review each frame before leaving it.

## INSERT A PERIOD; THEN WRITE IN A SUBJECT FOR THE SECOND SENTENCE

| | |
|---|---|
| . . . the cathode ray tube. (and) ✓ the electronic. . . . <br> . . . the cathode ray tube. The electronic. . . . | The size of the set depends on the size of the cathode ray tube, *and* the electronic packages affect the size of the smallest sets only. |
| . . . an 8-in-1 cabinet. (which) ✓ houses . . . <br> . . . an 8-in-1 cabinet. It houses . . . | The synchronizer cabinet is an 8-in-1 cabinet *which houses* two identical synchronizers and their switching and monitoring circuits. (Use it.") |
| . . . each function. (and) ✓ contain. . . . <br> each function. They contain. . . . | The tables give the order for testing each function *and contain* the following information: (Use "They.") |
| . . . system. (which) ✓ was based on <br> . . . system. This system (It) assumes . . . | In 1960, members of our research laboratories designed and built an infrared imaging system *which* assumes the principle of varying absorption of infrared light by changing the free-carrier density in a silicon filter. (Use "This system.") |
| . . . through a clutch (that) disengages. . . . <br> . . . through a clutch. This clutch disengages. . . . | This potentiometer connects to the azimuth-sector assembly through a clutch *that* disengages the potentiometer whenever the sector selector disengages from the relay receiver. (Use "This clutch.") |
| . . . the secondary. (which) ✓ <br> . . . the secondary. This resistance absorbs. . . . | An important feature of this rectifier design is the thyrite resistance across each phase of the secondary *which* absorbs transient voltages that otherwise would weaken the silicon diodes. (Use "This resistance.") |
| . . . to the C axis. for (which) ✓ light . . . <br> . . . to the C axis. For this light . . . | The darker image was produced by light polarized parallel to the C axis, *for which* light the absorption edge is deeper in the red end of the spectrum. (Use "For this.") |
| . . . the infrared detector. (and) ✓ operates like. . . . <br> . . . the infrared detector. It operates like. . . . | The temperature controller is near the infrared detector *and* operates like a thermistor. (Use "It.") |

## SUBORDINATE THE SECOND SENTENCE OR SECOND ELEMENT BY CHANGING ITS VERB TO AN "-ING" FORM

| | |
|---|---|
| . . . , the only exceptions *being* the oscilloscopes.<br><br>(except for the oscilloscopes.) | The test equipment for each radio is identical. The only exceptions *are* the oscilloscopes. (Use "being.") |
| . . . tube, (and) the electronic packages *affecting* the size of the. . . . | The size of the set depends on the size of the cathode ray tube, and the electronic packages *affect* the size of the smallest sets only. |
| . . . capacity, (and) thereby *improving* the. . . . | The additional reflectivity doubled the light-gathering capacity and thereby *improved* the signal-to-noise ratio. |
| . . . a gray-scale image, (and) presenting it. . . . | These techniques take the first or the second isotropic derivative of a gray-scale image and present it as a black-and-white image. |

Subordinate in the following sentences the ideas connected with the first verb:

## SUBORDINATE IN APPOSITION THE IDEA FOLLOWING THE FIRST VERB

| | |
|---|---|
| This chapter, which is divided into two sections, contains . . . | This chapter *is divided into two sections and* contains information on maintaining the synchronizer.<br><br>This chapter, which |
| The preamplifier, which has two differential amplifier stages, provides a. . . . | The preamplifier *has two differential amplifier stages and* provides a gain of 40 decibels.<br><br>The preamplifier, |
| The tables, which are organized . . . of testing, contain. . . . | The tables *are organized in the order of testing and* contain the following information:<br><br>The tables, |

## SUBORDINATE IN APPOSITION THE IDEA FOLLOWING THE SECOND VERB

| | |
|---|---|
| A separate gating circuit, described in Appendix C, can remove this noise. | A separate gating circuit can remove this noise. This gating circuit is described in Appendix C.<br><br>A separate gating circuit, |

| | |
|---|---|
| This study, which has already begun, should be. . . . | This study should be well advanced by that time. It has already begun. |
| | This study, |
| Hawser force tests, mentioned in the paper about the Dallas Dam, were made in the. . . . | Hawser force tests were made in the prototype. These were mentioned in the paper about the Dallas Dam. |
| | Hawser force tests, |
| The fluid pump, which consists of two . . . systems, provides. . . . | The fluid pump provides mobile power and consists of two independent systems. |
| | The fluid pump, which |

COMMENT: THOUGH SECONDARY ELEMENTS SHOULD BE IN FORMS SHOWING THEIR SUBORDINATE STATUS, ELEMENTS THAT HAVE EQUAL VALUE SHOULD SHOW THEIR PARALLEL STATUS. IN THE FOLLOWING SENTENCE THE FORM OF "ARRANGING" IMPLIES THAT ARRANGING IS SUBORDINATE TO CHECKING:

The printer controller *checks* each character for parity, *arranging* them in a line of 120 characters.

BUT CHECKING AND ARRANGING ARE INDEPENDENT OPERATIONS; NEITHER IS SECONDARY TO THE OTHER. THEIR INDEPENDENT AND PARALLEL STANDING CAN BE BROUGHT OUT BY CHANGING BOTH WORDS INTO PRESENT-TENSE VERBS:

The printer controller *checks* each character for parity and *arranges* them in a line of 120 characters.

THE PARALLEL STATUS OF EVEN INDIVIDUAL WORDS CAN BE SHOWN BY GIVING THEM SIMILAR FORMS, FOR EXAMPLE, BY GIVING THEM SIMILAR ENDINGS, AS IN:

These tables contain the data for clean*ing,* inspec*tion*(ing), and lubricat*ing.*

AND IN:

This manual contains the information needed for troubleshoot*ing,* align*ment of* (aligning), and test*ing* the *discriminator.*

CHAPTER HEADINGS AND ITEMS IN LISTS USUALLY ARE SIMILAR IN VALUE; SO THEY ARE NATURALS FOR PARALLEL FORM, AS IN:

1. *Clean* cabinet and console
2. *Clean* print characters
3. Latch and hinge inspection and lubrication. (*Inspect* and *lubricate* latch and hinge.)

AND IN:

1. Start-power application
2. Indication of switching complete (Switching-complete indication)
3. Full-speed power application

or

1. Application of. . . .
2. Indication of. . . .
3. Application of. . . .

# LIGHTENING UNIT MODIFIERS AND LOCATING MODIFIERS EFFECTIVELY

**16**

We have already hyphened unit modifiers. We can now see how to break these modifiers into lighter, more easily comprehensible units. Then we will also see how to position sentence elements effectively.

## 16-1 Lightening Unit Modifiers with Prepositions

While hyphening does clarify the relation between modifier and modified, the hyphened expression often remains an overweight conglomeration of ideas, as in the plodding:

**The pedestal-power-disconnect-contact relay.**

This is just too much information. You can break up overweight unit modifiers with prepositions such as "of," "for," and "on." These will also show the exact relationship of the words. An expression such as:

**A mixed-mail deck**

can become:

**A deck** *of* **mixed mail**

The hyphen is no longer needed, since the preposition "of" now links the two words of the modifier, "mixed mail."

### In Phrases

Shift modifiers around similarly in the following phrases. Remove the hyphen, and use the suggested word as the link.

### LIGHTEN WITH SUGGESTED WORDS

| | |
|---|---|
| The polarity *of the* input signal | The input-signal polarity |
| | The polarity *of the* |
| The voltage check *for the* power supply | The power-supply voltage check |
| | The voltage check *for the* |
| The selection *of the* tuning method (Selecting the. . . .) | The tuning-method selection (of the) |
| | The selection |
| The ripple check in the power supply | The power-supply ripple check (in the) |
| | The ripple check |
| The bypass *of the* interlock *on the* control panel | The control-panel interlock bypass (of the, on the) |
| | The bypass of the _____ on the |
| The title *of the* field of interest | The field-of-interest title (of the) |
| | The title |
| For use *of the* Government Purchasing Office | For Government Purchasing Office use (of the) |
| | For use |
| | (Proper names are not hyphened.) |

COMMENT: YOU CAN SEE HOW THESE REVISIONS CAN MORE EXACTLY BRING OUT RELATIONSHIPS BY CONSIDERING THE FOLLOWING FAIRLY STRAIGHTFORWARD EXPRESSION:

Wall-mounted receptacles

THIS COULD MEAN ANY OF THE FOLLOWING:

Receptacles mounted *on* $\left(\begin{array}{l}\text{in, into, at, across, by, from, around, behind, down, inside,} \\ \text{through, within, etc.)}\end{array}\right.$ the wall

THESE PREPOSITIONS PICTURE THE RECEPTACLES WITH RESPECT TO THE WALL, WHICH IS SOMETHING HYPHENS CANNOT DO.

| | |
|---|---|
| The timing checks *for the* core memory | The core-memory timing checks |
| | (for the) |
| | The timing checks |

| | |
|---|---|
| Cleaning *the* interior *of the* manual-input consolette | The manual-input consolette-interior cleaning |
| | Cleaning *the* _____ *of the* manual-input consolette |
| The encoding *of* clipped speech *into* symbols | The clipped-speech, symbol encoding |
| | The encoding *of* _____ *into* symbols |
| The modified circuits *in the* pitch extractor | The modified pitch-extractor circuits |
| | (in the) |
| | The modified circuits |
| A simulation *of* voice *at a* low bit rate | A low bit-rate voice simulation |
| | A simulation *of* _____ at a low _____ . |
| The waveform generator *for (the)* formant control. | The formant-control waveform generator |
| | (for the) |
| | The waveform generator |
| Our word boards *for the* city-state recognizer. | Our city-state recognizer word boards |
| | (for the) |
| | Our word boards _____ city state |

### In Sentences

The unit modifiers are in sentences in the following frames:

*REWRITE UNIT MODIFIERS, USUALLY WITH "OF THE" OR "THAT"*

| | |
|---|---|
| . . . the concentration *of (the)* donor impurity. | $N_0$ is the donor-impurity concentration. |
| | $N_0$ is the concentration |
| . . . on the progress *of the* maintenance program. | Please forward all reports on the maintenance-program progress. |
| | . . . on the progress |
| . . . to the width *of the* sector scan. | The voltage is proportional to the sector-scan width. |
| | . . . to the |

| | |
|---|---|
| The time *for the* absorption change depends on the intensity *of the* incident light. | The absorption-change time depends on incident-light intensity. |
| | The time *for the* _____ depends on the _____ *of the* |
| . . . the level *of the* input carrier | Decrease the input-carrier level. |
| | . . . decrease the |
| . . . the dominant mechanism *for* (*in*) scattering *at* low temperature. | This factor is the dominant low-temperature scattering mechanism. |
| | . . . is the dominant _____ *for* scattering *at* |
| . . . are devices *for* reduction *of* speech bandwidth. (for reducing) | Vocoders are speech-bandwidth reduction devices. (for, of) |
| | . . . are devices |
| . . . emphasizes encoding *at* high speed and *with* high precision. | Their design emphasizes high-speed and high-precision encoding. |
| | . . . emphasizes _____ *at* _____ *and with* |
| . . . feeds circuits *that* sample *the* antenna excitation. | This input feeds antenna-excitation sampler circuits. |
| | . . . feeds circuits *that* _____ *the* |
| . . . tests *of* voice quality *and* intelligibility. | We are now conducting voice quality and intelligibility tests. |
| | . . . conducting tests *of* _____ *and* |
| . . . a facility manual *for the* check-out set. | This is a check-out set facility manual. (for the) |
| | This is a facility manual |

COMMENT: THOUGH IT IS USUALLY GOOD TO LIGHTEN THE TEXT WITH PREPOSITIONS, YOU SHOULDN'T OVERUSE THEM, AS IN:

The maintenance table lists the *points of test*.

"TEST POINTS" WILL DO. SIMILARLY IN:

This program shows the *points of lubrication*.

"LUBRICATION POINTS" WILL DO.

## 16-2   Relocating Ineffectively Placed Expressions

By simply shifting some expressions you can avoid much ambiguity.

### Simple Relocations

Connections between related expressions should be obvious. In the following sentence "only" relates to either "printer" or to "power washer."

Place the stripped printer (only) in the power washer.

"Only" squints; that is, it looks in two directions because of its placement. The writer intended to say:

Place *only* the printer in the . . . washer.

which is how he should have written it, but, as written, it also suggests:

Place the . . . printer in the washer *only.*

Other misplaced expressions are italicized in the following sentences. Draw an arrow from them to a more effective location. To be sure your relocation is fitting, reread the sentence before checking left. Then review the frame before leaving it.

---

*DRAW ARROWS TO MORE EFFECTIVE POSITIONS FOR ITALICIZED EXPRESSIONS*

---

| | |
|---|---|
| Modules, (after checkout), will be encapsulated. | Modules, *after checkout,* will be encapsulated. |
| Program the concentrator, to detect (beforehand) . . . | Program the concentrator to detect *beforehand* when data exceeds capacity. |
| Gallium arsenide is (only) known to crystallize in the cubic. . . . | Gallium arsenide is *only* known to crystallize in the cubic zinc blende structure. |
| A (permanently) technician is assigned to maintain . . . | A *permanent* technician is assigned to maintain the computer. (Use "permanently.") |
| . . . low-zinc . . . films have not been (satisfactory) produced. | Because of their limited resolution, low-zinc composition films have not been *satisfactorily* produced. ("Satisfactorily" becomes "satisfactory.") |

### Modifiers at Ends of Sentences

The writers of the following sentences placed expressions ineffectively at their end. Seemingly, they tacked them on as an afterthought. Place them more effectively in the body of the sentence, not at the beginning of the sentence.

After you circle the expression, check at the upper left to be sure you have circled all of it. Before checking at the lower left, reread the sentence as you have revised it.

## *CIRCLE AND RELOCATE MISPLACED EXPRESSIONS*

titled "Self-compensating Triangulator Rangefinder"

He presented a paper at the. . . .

(At the . . . he presented a . . . titled. . . .)

He presented a paper at the Tenth Annual Military Electronics Convention *titled "Self-compensating Triangulator Rangefinder."*

---

and its automatic checkout systems *were*

Sideswiper was designed. . . .

Sideswiper was designed and manufactured by our company and its automatic checkout systems. (Change the form of "was.")

---

for digitally encoding the signal

Other techniques will also be. . . .

Other techniques will also be considered for digitally encoding the signal.

---

simultaneously

The six networks match the data. . . .

The six networks match the data in the register against the data in the six channels *simultaneously.*

---

for converting . . . two-level waveform

A half-dozen techniques have been given. . . .

A half-dozen techniques have been given in the preceding sections for converting analog speech into an intelligible two-level waveform.

---

any spray

The vent plug returns to the cell.

The vent plug returns to the cell *any spray.*

---

a set of instructions

A subroutine *inserts* in the. . . .

A subroutine inserts in the compiled program a set of instructions.

---

several outputs

This subroutine extracts from a. . . .

This subroutine extracts from a single file several outputs.

| | |
|---|---|
| [by standard techniques] Equilibrium is difficult to attain in these. . . . | Equilibrium is difficult to attain in these strongly banded III-IV structures *by standard techniques.* |
| , [when the project is starting,] Another important consideration is that our department will be. . . . | Another important consideration is that our department will be completing two projects nearby *when this project is starting.* |
| , [by clipping,] . . . take the derivative and represent it as a. . . . | These techniques take the derivative and represent it as a gray-scale image or a black-and-white image *by clipping.* |

### Moving Modifiers to the Beginning of the Sentence

The misplaced expressions in most of the following sentences affect the thought of the entire sentence. For this reason they belong at or near the start of the sentence. This applies to logical connectives, such as "however," "therefore," and "on the other hand"; but these usually work better inside the sentence, usually after the first significant expression.

*CIRCLE MISPLACED EXPRESSIONS AND RELOCATE THEM, USUALLY AT THE BEGINNING OF THE SENTENCE*

| | |
|---|---|
| [as a result of unrecorded observations] We believe . . . | We believe the other types of bulbs have shorter relaxation times, as a result of unrecorded observations. |
| [as experiments show] Much smaller differences. . . . | Much smaller differences in atomic radii can be tolerated, as experiments show. |
| [however] Chemical and structural considerations impose other limitations. | Chemical and structural considerations impose other limitations, *however*, with the result that Ag is the most likely substitute. |
| [with the four-bit system] Experienced persons consistently averaged higher . . . | Experienced persons consistently averaged higher, and inexperienced persons consistently averaged lower *with the four-bit system.* |
| [therefore] Epitaxy should occur when films of. . . . | Epitaxy should therefore occur when films of mixed crystals are deposited. |

| | |
|---|---|
| ⌐in the processor⌐ | The master trigger generates delay times equivalent to 5,000, 10,000, and 15,000 meters in the processor. |
| The master trigger generates delay times, equivalent to. . . . | |

COMMENT: SOMETIMES THE READER CAN RELOCATE IMPROPERLY PLACED EXPRESSIONS BUT NOT ALWAYS. FOR EXAMPLE, ONLY THE WRITER OF THE FOLLOWING SENTENCE COULD KNOW WHAT "IF DESIRED" FITS WITH:

The computer generates one or more output tapes and a console-typewriter output, *if desired.*

THIS MOST LIKELY MEANS THAT, IF DESIRED, THE COMPUTER CAN GENERATE A TYPEWRITER OUTPUT. BUT, TOO, IT MIGHT MEAN THAT, IF DESIRED, THE COMPUTER CAN GENERATE OUTPUT TAPES. AND IT MIGHT ALSO MEAN THAT, UNLESS DESIRED, THE COMPUTER WILL GENERATE NEITHER. THE WRITER, OF COURSE, KNOWS, BUT WE READERS CANNOT KNOW WHAT HE INTENDED. IT MIGHT EVEN BE THAT HE SHOULD HAVE ENTIRELY OMITTED "IF DESIRED."

## 16-3 Review

Lighten unit modifiers in the following frames. Use the suggested words, and remove hyphens.

| | |
|---|---|
| The signal *that has* two levels | The two-level signal |
| | The signal *that has* |
| with a deck *of* mixed mail | With a mixed-mail deck |
| | With a deck *of* |
| A pitch extractor *for the* time domain | A time-domain pitch extractor |
| | (for the) |
| | A pitch extractor |
| For alignment *of the* high-voltage protection circuit. | For high-voltage protection-circuit alignment (of the) |
| | For alignment _____ high-voltage |
| The lattice parameters calculated *for* differing compositions. | The differing-compositions, calculated lattice parameters |
| | The lattice parameters calculated *for* |
| For alignment *of the* logic chassis (for aligning the logic chassis) | For logic-chassis alignment (of the) |
| | For alignment |
| . . . the information *about* (the) zero crossings | This retains the zero-crossing information (about) |

| | |
|---|---|
| Knobs are coded *by* shape. | The knobs are shape-coded. (by) |
| . . . mounted *on the* front panel. | The circuit breakers are front-panel-mounted. (on the) |
| . . . pulse width *of the* radar transmitter. | Calculate the radar-transmitter pulse width. (of the) |
| Inspect and clean the faces *of* the release cam. | Inspect and clean the release-cam faces. (of) |
| . . . a signal *that has* high amplitude *and* low frequency | We must add a high-amplitude, low-frequency signal (that has, and) |
| Test under conditions *of* partial failure. | Test under partial-failure conditions. (of) |
| . . . information *about* the class of service at this time. | It stores the class-of-service information at this time. |
| | . . . information *about* the |
| . . . a high ratio *of* capacitative reactance to inductive reactance. | These circuits have a high capacitive-reactance to inductive-reactance ratio. |
| | . . . have a high ratio of _____ to |
| . . . the output keys *to* (*for, of*) *the* alarm signal. | This signal activates the alarm-signal output keys. (to the) |
| | . . . activates the output keys to the |
| . . . the power *of the* exciting light. | The change in transmission depends on the exciting-light power. (of the) |
| | . . . depends on the |
| . . . to components *for the* computer system. (for computer systems) | These range from module cards to computer-system components. |
| | . . . from module cards to _____ for the _____ . |
| Thus, at higher levels *of* current density | Thus, at higher current-density levels we can learn $T_{ec}$ by the following formula: |
| | Thus, at higher levels of |
| Section IV details procedures for removal and for preparation for shipment. | Section IV details removal-and-preparation-for-shipment procedures. |
| | . . . details procedures for _____ and for |

The following frames have ineffectively placed expressions.

## CIRCLE MISPLACED EXPRESSIONS; THEN RELOCATE THEM

| | |
|---|---|
| The traffic capacity of thirty loops (or more) was. . . . | The traffic capacity of thirty loops *or more* was the basis of comparison. |
| We have used. . . . (successfully.) | We have used a two-beam, optical interference detector *successfully*. |
| . . . the electronic packages (only) limit the overall dimensions, for the smallest modules. | The sizes of the electronic packages *only* limit the overall dimensions for the smallest modules. |
| Circuit breakers are (all) . . . | Circuit breakers are *all* adjacent to the front panel. |
| The average evaporation rate is, (however,) more. . . . | The average evaporation rate is, *however*, more rigidly controlled. |
| . . . is the number of times a second the voltage changes . . . | The frequency is the number of times the voltage changes from positive to negative *a second*. |
| The new stripper was then built and tested, (which is shown in) (Figure 2,) | The new stripper was then built and tested *which is shown in Figure 2*. |
| One air conditioner can (normally) maintain. . . . | One air conditioner can *normally* maintain the listed temperature and humidity. |
| Graded-composition diodes been made (ranging from) (. . . to . . . ZnS.) | Graded-composition diodes have been made *ranging from 0 to 5 percent and 0 to 30 percent ZnS*. |
| Each trunk group appears green, yellow, red, and blinking red, as the . . . degrades (successively.) | Each trunk group appears green, yellow, red, and blinking red as the trunk capability degrades *successively*. |
| This signal punches a tape in the . . . (with its own routing,) | This signal punches a tape in the torn-tape room *with its own routing*. |
| A method of tracking has been developed . . . , (which correlates . . . incoming data,) | A method of tracking has been developed in our laboratories *which correlates the contents of a magnetic-drum memory with incoming data*. |
| A second modification, was added . . . , (which increased) (reliability.) | A second modification was added to the motor controller, *which increased reliability*. |

| | |
|---|---|
| Experiments are underway to increase . . . rate. | Experiments are underway *to increase further the energy discharge rate.* |
| Using a . . . as a leak detector, *we detected no leaks.* | There were no detectable leaks using a helium mass spectrometer as a leak detector. (Rewrite with ''we.'') |

## RECOMMENDED BOOKS

### The following are brief, to the point, and rich in content:

*Writing a Technical Paper,* Menzel, Donald H., Jones, Howard Mumford, and Boyd, Lyle G., McGraw-Hill Book Company, New York, 1961 (128 pages).

Excellent. Written by knowledgeable scientists.

*The Elements of Style,* Strunk, Wm., Jr., and White, E. B., The Macmillan Company, 1959 (71 pages).

A classic, updated.

*Clarity in Technical Reporting,* Katzoff, S., U.S. Government Printing Office, Washington, D.C. (25 pages). For sale by the Superintendent of Documents, U.S. Government Printing Office, Washington, D.C. 20402 (15 cents).

Originally an informal, internal paper at Langley Research Center in NASA, this pithy booklet earned recognition by word of mouth.

*Gobbledygook Has Gotta Go,* O'Hayre, John, U.S. Government Printing Office, Washington, D.C. (112 pages). For sale by the Superintendent of Documents, U.S. Government Printing Office, Washington, D.C. 20402, 40 cents.

Essays against ''officialese,'' by an employee of the Bureau of Land Management.

*Plain Style,* Durham, John, and Zall, Paul, McGraw-Hill Book Company, New York, 1967 (225 pages).

Not directed at technical writers, and some of the examples are adolescent, but its graphic highlighting of paragraph and essay development make this an invaluable help for anyone having difficulty organizing ideas.

*The Golden Book on Writing,* Lambuth, David, and others, The Viking Press, Inc., New York, 1964 (81 pages).

Includes advice for those with mental blocks against writing.

**The following are longer but filled with many and extended illustrations of the principles of clear, direct writing:**

*The Technique of Clear Writing,* Gunning, Robert, McGraw-Hill Book Company, New York, 1968 (revised edition).

Includes his Fog Index, a readability yardstick. Also has a thirteen-page list of short substitutes for overweight words. He has taught his ten principles in many corporations, newspapers, The Associated Press, and United Press International.

*How to Write, Speak, and Think More Effectively,* Flesch, Rudolf, Harper & Row, Publishers, Incorporated, New York, 1960.

Flesch's readability test includes a score for human interest in addition to one for reading ease.

*The Language of Science: A Guide to Effective Writing,* Gilman, William, Harcourt, Brace & World, Inc., New York, 1961.

**Here are some alphabetically arranged reference works:**

*The ABC of Style: A Guide to Plain English,* Flesch, Rudolf, Harper & Row, Publishers, Incorporated, New York, 1964.

A word dictionary for the verbally overweight.

*The Careful Writer: A Modern Guide to English Usage,* Bernstein, Theodore M., Atheneum Publishers, New York, 1965.

A more traditional viewpoint written while assistant managing editor of *The New York Times.*

*Writer's Guide and Index to English,* 4th ed., Perrin, Porter G., Scott, Foresman and Company, Glenview, Ill., 1966.

An outstanding English textbook in addition to the index.

Gold mines of information but more complex than the preceding are the preeminent Henry W. Fowler's classic: *A Dictionary of Modern English Usage;* its simplified American adaptation: *A Dictionary of American English Usage* by Margaret Nicholson; and Eric Partridge's *Usage and Abusage.*

Harry Golden, in his book *Carl Sandburg,* wrote "Carl was always reading. One of the pure joys for me in writing this book has been the satisfaction in confirming a pet theory of mine: that you cannot be a writer unless you are a reader. First a child must hear before he can speak, and first a writer must read before he can write." *Carl Sandburg,* The World Publishing Co., Cleveland, Ohio, 1961.

Do your reading by studying masterpieces of English prose. Read W. Somerset Maugham, Sinclair Lewis, Bertrand Russell, and George Orwell. Read Hemingway and John Steinbeck. Read some of the better magazines, such as *Harper's Magazine* and *The Atlantic*. Observe how *Scientific American* presents technical material for its untrained audience. At any rate, read and read.

Don't read passively. Sometimes read aloud: listen to the flow of the words and to the rhythm. Other times observe how the author develops an idea. Then pay attention to the vocabulary. Next attend to the punctuation. You may find it rewarding to read a single page five or six times, with a different viewpoint each time.

If you want more technical readings, try some of the following:

*Readings for Technical Writers,* Blickle, Margaret D., and Passe, Martha E., Ronald Press Company, New York, 1963.

*Classics in Science,* Philosophical Library, Inc., New York, 1960.

*Scientists as Writers,* Harrison, James, editor, The M.I.T. Press, Cambridge, Mass., 1965.

*The Autobiography of Science,* Moulton, Forest Ray, and Schifferes, Justus J., editors, Doubleday & Company, Inc., Garden City, N.Y., 1960 (Second Edition)

**You will find many satisfactory textbooks on technical and report writing in bookstores and on library shelves. Since each author has directed his text to a specific audience and written from his own point of view, look over a few before you make a final selection. The following are mentioned, with the knowledge that others are unfairly of necessity omitted.**

*A Technical Writer's Handbook,* Norgaard, Margaret, Harper & Row, Publishers, Incorporated, New York, 1959.

*Technical Reporting,* Ulman, Joseph N., Jr., and Gould, Jay R., Holt, Rinehart and Winston, New York, 1959.

*Successful Technical Writing,* Hicks, Tyler G., McGraw-Hill Book Company, New York, 1959.

*Technical Writing,* Mills, G. H., and Walter, John A., Holt, Rinehart and Winston, Inc., New York, 1962.

*Basic Technical Writing,* Weisman, Herman M., Charles E. Merrill Books, Inc., Columbus, Ohio, 1968.

*A Guide to Technical Writing,* Crouch, George W., and Zetler, Robert L., The Ronald Press Company, New York, 1964.